The Future of Fundraising

How Philanthropy's Future is Here with Donors Dictating the Terms

Paul D'Alessandro, J.D., CFRE

High Impact Publishing

Published by High Impact Publishing
785 Franklin Avenue, Unit #749, Franklin Lakes, NJ 07417

ISBN: 978-1-7366647-0-4

DEDICATION

To my family, friends, and everyone who has ever wanted to make an impact on the world and live a life of purpose.

TABLE OF CONTENTS

INTRODUCTION

"Wealth is not new. Neither is charity. But the idea of using private wealth imaginatively, constructively and systematically to attack the fundamental problems of mankind is new." — John Gardner

"A.I. fundraising platform boodleAI has helped nonprofits acquire a $1,000 new donor in 10 minutes, raise $3,600 in new donors in one hour, raise $10,000 in new donations in one week and achieve email donation rates 100 times the average."[1] So wrote Shawn Olds for an article in *Nonprofit Pro*. If that doesn't convey the immense disruption and evolution happening in the nonprofit sector, I don't know what will.

There was a time when the issues faced by large nonprofits, medium, and small ones, were mostly unrelated. However, in many respects, that's changed. Today, what affects the large chapter organization with hundreds of millions of dollars in annual revenue may well also affect Main Street's small nonprofit. As an example, the pace in the change of technology is one thing that readily comes to mind. Another example is the 2020 pandemic and economic crisis. Nonprofit organizations did not get spared from these twin events.

Nevertheless, the reality is that change is continual, and disruptions can happen at any time. The unexpected is another thing large and small nonprofits and fundraisers have to contend with at any time. Also, the global public's push to see more equity and fairness is yet another thing that the large national group and the one-person nonprofit both experience. These are just a few quick examples of the realities and conversations gripping the nonprofit sector at every level. Because of it, fundraisers, nonprofit leaders, and volunteers have no choice to adapt to continual transformation and reinvention.

Fundraising has always been about connecting donors with a cause. I've long thought that there is plenty of money to solve many of the problems of the world. That may be why I entered into the fundraising

---

1 "Can Artificial Intelligence Really Accelerate Your Nonprofit's Mission?," Shawn Olds, Nonprofit Pro, August 27, 2019, https://www.nonprofitpro.com/article/can-artificial-intelligence-really-accelerate-your-nonprofits-mission/

field. I'm someone who cares about social good. As a result, I figured that I would do my part to help direct funds where they are needed so that donors, investors, and organizations could make the most significant impact.

Yet, despite the global wealth and the reality that we have the financial resources to ease or eliminate many of the world's problems, challenges remain. Understanding these obstacles and opportunities to improve lives will make people who do what I do better at our fundraising jobs in the 21st Century.

As an example, there's a challenge of directing fundraising dollars to where it's needed most. Some people want to focus on the most pressing priorities, and so they ask many questions. However, is eradicating poverty more important than ensuring the preservation of global heritage sites for future generations? Is curing cancer more important than, say, ensuring every child has a quality education?

These are philosophical questions, but because donors have different interests, sometimes there seems to be a lack of concerted will. Ultimately, everything comes at a cost, as we see with the global climate crisis that disproportionately affects people who live in poverty. Still, do people in the U.S. or Europe, for instance, want to truly get to net-zero greenhouse emissions if it means significantly curbing modern conveniences, such as air travel? Let us be mindful of the seemingly endless catastrophic events that happen globally, requiring immediate resources, as we've seen from natural disasters, a pandemic, and economic meltdowns.

Although there might be tensions on the collective will to prioritize anything, I think the global public's desire to see systemic change remains a reality. Still, competing interests from individuals and families, governments, businesses, etc., exist as to what gets designated as a top priority and what doesn't. Even though these are issues beyond my knowledge, and probably that of most fundraisers, merely being aware of them will make us all better fundraisers. As a result of understanding the broader context, we will internalize the idea that nothing is really "that simple."

The World Facing Fundraisers

We've gotten to the point where nonprofit donors, stakeholders, investors, and the public support their favorite causes every year. Each year, a bit of progress occurs, but then another fundraising message gets sent asking for another round of donations because the problem isn't entirely solved. Today's donors are sophisticated, including low dollar contributors and the young Generation Z, an activist group.

Because of the digital world, information travels around the world in seconds. That incredible power and access to all the world's knowledge make it much harder for nonprofit leaders and fundraisers to keep doing what they've been doing for years. The public and donors want change (even if they might disagree on what must change and how). Again, how much or what change is debatable. Nevertheless, what is a fact is that there is an unprecedented demand to make things better for people, especially as the world and nonprofits[2] move past COVID-19 and the massive loss of jobs. Also, because much of the public no longer trust that nonprofits[3]or governments can solve intractable social issues; they're pressing for-profit corporations and businesses to lead on social change.

So, we are now living in a time of immense disruption for a variety of reasons. It's not just because technology is evolving at an unprecedented rate that things change and evolve at an unprecedented pace. It's also because the global population has become impatient with talk when it sees that change can and should happen. Thus, the public demand that money and time, and that of governments, businesses, and nonprofits go to good use that makes a significant change. Of course, we also had a pandemic, and downturn results in the economy that has caused great harm. All of these situations and more inevitably mean that nonprofits must step up their game.

There was a time, I remember, when major donors and nonprofit leaders would sit around and discuss ideas of "closing the nonprofit." That was a quaint notion, but it's where we are heading. What those earlier donors and nonprofit leaders meant by the idea of closing nonprofits was that with good intentions, they wanted to close nonprofit doors—or see duplicated efforts consolidated.

Many thought that within a specific time frame, they would ensure humans would never have to suffer or experience whatever the mission was trying to solve. Still, conversations about closures, partnerships, and mergers eventually fell away, and nonprofits became big business,[4] collectively speaking. Americans give more than $427.71 billion in 2018 to char-

2 "The CARES Act: What the New Economic Stimulus Package Means for Your Charitable Giving at NCF," National Christian Foundation, April 2020, https://www.ncfgiving.com/wp-content/uploads/2020/04/The-CARES-Act-What-it-means-for-your-giving-with-NCF.pdf

3 "Better Business Bureau," Give.org, January 31, 2018, http://www.give.org/news-updates/2018/01/31/wise-giving-wednesday-drop-in-trust-in-non-profit-organizations-in-u.s

4 "The Charitable Sector," Independent Sector, https://independentsector.org/about/the-charitable-sector/

ity,[5] and that number only reflects money reported from tax data. Also, more than 63 million volunteers help out at 1.6 million nonprofits across the country. In other words, that's a lot of money and people heading into the social good sector.

In addition to the will to act, to make sure we solve at least some of the world's challenges so that nonprofits can be more strategic is the fact that we have to find the right way to do it. Consequently, nonprofits have to create the vehicles to address, but it also has to happen cost-effectively. We know there are vast wealth resources worldwide, but no one wants to invest in programs that will never succeed.

That said, stakeholders, including donors and investors, are willing to invest in well-thought-out, measurable, and results-driven pilots or plans that will *significantly* move the needle. So, while people understand that change comes in steps, the steps have to be broader and deeper than they were in the past. Thus, money has to be spent well and cost-effectively for more considerable results-driven investments into solutions. People want change, but because money does have value, that change has to be cost-effective.

Although this book focuses on the changing landscape of fundraising, I think it's important to mention the challenges that force fundraising to change from what it was in the past. When you are aware and understand the deeper issues and concerns of donors, investors, and key stakeholders, you can better navigate the fundraising world. As an example, the next time you're sitting with a major donor, you'll have a better handle of not only their giving to your group but also what their broader philanthropic thinking may be.

With donors and investors, it always comes down to the most effective use of time and money. With over 1.6 million charities in the United States alone, it is hard to conceive, but there remains a lack of ideas to address the most critical problems. Perhaps there has been a lack of consistent and robust will in the philanthropic community, government, and the public. Alternately, maybe there wasn't the ability to invest in technology and tools—until now—that could significantly improve lives.

No matter why, we know that we've entered over the threshold of a brave new world for everyone. For better or worse, the 21st Century, with its technology and disruptive change because of more exceptional abilities

---

5 Giving USA, 2019, https://givingusa.org/giving-usa-2019-americans-gave-427-71-billion-to-charity-in-2018-amid-complex-year-for-charitable-giving/

and data information, has already brought immense change, including to us fundraisers. Now, we have to harness that power for even more effective good. Fundraisers could be some of the leaders of this new disruptive era because they serve as the bridge between donors and investors' interest and intentions and the organizations (for-profit or nonprofit) that can get it done.

While disruption happens on a global and societal scale that affects all nonprofits, there remains one fundraising consistency. That's the fact donors continue to drive the conversation on how to solve many of our social problems. By the way, when I speak of donors, I'm not just referring to major donors who give thousands or millions of dollars. I'm also talking about the collective power of the low dollar donors who leverage their generosity in the digital world.

Because of the capabilities of technology, their voices are only going to get louder. Therefore, nonprofit leaders—and fundraisers especially—have no choice but to pay attention. Still, I hope that the philanthropic sector becomes more of a meaningful partnership between nonprofit leaders with talent, information, and ideas and their supporters. charity: water is an excellent example of that innovation coming not from donors pushing leaders but from the inside of the organization out to society. In other words, the charity: water team is leading the global discussion about clean water.

Donors Underwrite What They Help Write

I've been a professional fundraising consultant and strategist for over 30 years. Moreover, I've paid close attention to the over 4,000 donors I've met with during that time. One of the main lessons I've learned is that the axiom, "donors underwrite what they help write," is correct. Donors and investors who are engaged in the process of change will fund what they hope to change. A wise nonprofit leader has to understand that's the way it should be (it is their money, after all).

Nonprofit leaders should absorb the fact that they are not in charge of fundraising; the donors' interest dictates that. I think in many ways, fundraisers understand this reality. Nevertheless, it's more challenging for other nonprofit people—particularly in smaller nonprofits where there's a lot of passion—to wrap their heads around that idea. Meaning, nonprofits have to tell a compelling story that makes sense to donors and captures their imaginations that things can change for the better. That then gets proven with metrics and results.

Of course, nonprofit leaders and program professionals like to think they're on the leading edge of change or coming up with solutions to the world's problems. In many ways, it is their thinking and knowledge base that help inform donors and investors. However, it's the person with the money who decides what cause and program matters. Donors are directing where they want their charitable dollars to impact the U.S. and anywhere in the world significantly. It is that reality that, in turn, prioritizes how nonprofits will spend the contributions they receive.

For instance, if donors aren't interested in funding another after-school program in a community where there are five good ones, chances are it's not going to happen. Or, if donors want their funds directed to combat global climate change, that's where the money is going to go. Maybe within a few years, donors will decide that the genuinely innovative visionaries are not in the nonprofit sector but the for-profit world. They may begin to support businesses such as 4Ocean. In short, donors are investors, and the best nonprofits understand that concept.

As the disruption in the fundraising and nonprofit world continues, we also have to contend with businesses looking to maximize the reach to potential donors. The shift in business priorities and strategy began with cause-related marketing in making social good part of their culture to promote a greater good in society to the public.

In the intervening years, we saw communities where corporate employees live, to the consumers that use products from companies like Medtronic or Johnson & Johnson or American Express, enjoy the benefits of this positioning and message from Corporate America. Unfortunately, far away in foreign countries such as India or on the continents of Asia or Africa, employees for these corporations work for barely livable wages.

There are always competing interests, and you inevitably have counter-reaction to that kind of corporate strategy. For example, in 2019, the Business Roundtable, where JPMorgan Chase, Apple, Amazon, Walmart, and others are members, announced they would no longer prioritize shareholder profits exclusively. They also announced that companies would invest in professional development for their employees, the environment, and fair and equitable dealings with third-party vendors along with shareholder profits.

How this unfolds is already getting debated. Notably, while tens of millions have lost jobs, the stock market has not been affected negatively, showing what economists say that the stock market is not the economy. Nevertheless, it's the first time in decades that there's a discussion about corporations benefitting anyone else but shareholders.

Another counter-reaction is the creation of socially-minded for-profit businesses such as 4Ocean. They sell bracelets, and the profits get used to clean the ocean of plastics. In other words, here you have a for-profit company that is on the leading edge of social change for the environment, and they sell bracelets—and do not ask for donations.

If you think nonprofits are not innovating in this new environment, you are mistaken. You have organizations such as charity:water that created an employee incentive program called The Pool. The nonprofit wants to ensure it retains and compensates top talent well.

Nevertheless, this philosophy goes against what many in the industry believe: high nonprofit and performance pay is not appropriate. charity:water saw what's happening, and it decided to buck conventional nonprofit ideas. However, most nonprofits are not charity:water, but they could be if they thought innovatively and broke from thoughts of the past.

Disruption in Fundraising

One of the most remarkable fundraising experiences, and technological disruption, occurred with the ALS Ice Bucket Challenge[6]. It was one of the first examples I could think of where donors activated to support a cause, and artificial intelligence amplified the fundraising. Tina Zeff, Chief Operating Officer, The ALS Association, described what happened.

> *Immediately after the Ice Bucket Challenge, the organization wanted to focus on the power of individual giving. The Ice Bucket Challenge raised millions of dollars and flooded the organization with new individual donors. The Association wanted to harness the value of new individual supporters and turn them into lifetime donors. Not having the expertise or technology to do that, a new partnership formed with Mastercard, a consumer finance company. Mastercard came alongside ALS because they understood big data and the power of consumer engagement and took a look at the Association's data with a view into future opportunities. Within 48 hours, Mastercard was able to identify where the potential was for individual giving across the organization and was quickly able to see where other revenue and engagement opportunities could exist within the marketplace.*

I understand that the word "disruption" has become so common

---

6 "Ice Bucket Challenge," Wikipedia, https://en.wikipedia.org/wiki/Ice_Bucket_Challenge

as to be trite. However, if you don't think we have entered a new era of fundraising, I've got a bridge to sell you in Brooklyn. Everything evolves, and the digital world is disrupting every corner of society. Accordingly, that includes the nonprofit sector. It won't take you much effort to Google "disruption in the nonprofit sector" and see more than 4 million search results. In other words, it's an essential and much written about the topic.

The change provides charities resources and where business entities and initiatives get created to solve specific social problems. In other words, social changes are not only coming—as they have done in the past—through the work done within nonprofits.

In today's world, you also have social enterprises and even global corporations looking to lend a hand for social good. That means donors don't have only to support nonprofits to make a difference, which is a reason, for instance, that impact investing took off. Nonprofits must realize that donors (investors) have options to place their money for social change. It can go into a nonprofit or for-profit. The boundaries have gotten blurred, and now it's about who can create significant and scalable growth.

Fundraising has a trillion-dollar impact on our economy every year. It includes the more than $427.71 billion reflected in giving data from tax returns submitted in the U.S. from individuals. People want to impact the world in which they live and have looked to charities or other entities to help them accomplish that simple goal. They've served on boards, volunteered, and have been donors to nonprofit organizations. However, when nonprofits were almost exclusively, the only place a person or business could make a social impact or where the single revenue source was donor dollars has come to an end.

Instead, today, social good supporters and donors seek results, and they know they have options. Consequently, they're not patient enough to wait 5, 10, or 25 years to see change happen. People have been waiting hundreds, thousands, or even millennia to see poverty, diseases, and intractable social challenges come to an end. Governments can't seem to get it done because they are beholden to special interests. For example, we seem to be no better off in the "war against poverty" than when we started, which became apparent following the loss of jobs as commerce ground to a halt because of COVID-19. Technology, new ideas, innovations, and the resources available today will help ensure that the public and donors don't have to wait for more generations.

What's a Nonprofit Fundraising Leader to Do?

The time has arrived to prepare for the changes already impacting how we fundraise now and in the future. We must provide the resources to solve some of the challenges in the world. In particular, nonprofits need to look at revenue streams beyond the traditional methods that have worked for the last 70 years.

Therefore, in reading this book, we will explore the things that have and will have the most significant impact on the future of fundraising. When you complete the book, you'll understand why you should be looking to adapt to those changes for "high impact" instead of struggling for existence in an ever-changing environment.

In the following pages, you'll have my take and understanding of how artificial intelligence affects fundraising, for instance. You'll also get to read words from people in the industry and what they see happening for social good. We'll touch on issues that range from donor privacy to impact investing, blockchain philanthropy, and why we should end compensating fundraisers solely with fees or a salary. Yes, I've said it. Donors, including businesses, want to see pay for performance. Why shouldn't fundraisers earn a fee or salary and incentive money for performance?

We'll also tackle the reality that many nonprofits have to merge, collaborate more, consolidate, or perhaps even close. There is too much duplication with many charities operating on less than $100,000, which is not sustainable. Also, fewer than 25 percent of nonprofits[7] have less than six months operating revenue, which is dangerous in case of a significant economic downturn, such as what happened in 2008 and happened in 2020.

So, sit back, kick up your feet, and open your mind to a new reality of the future of fundraising. This book is your opportunity to join visionary fundraising leaders who seek to become the architects of the future of fundraising.

---

7   "Operating Reserves for Nonprofits," National Council of Nonprofits, https://www.councilofnonprofits.org/tools-resources/operating-reserves-nonprofits

ONE

ARTIFICIAL INTELLIGENCE AND ITS IMPACT ON SOCIETY

"…in this new age of AI, many time-honored assumptions about strategy and leadership no longer apply." — From the book, "Competing in the Age of AI: Strategy and Leadership When Algorithms and Networks Run the World" by Marco Iansiti and Karim R. Lakhanti

I started the Introduction of this book with a quote from Shawn Olds. So far, it's the most succinct explanation about what's happening in the fundraising world because of the power of artificial intelligence (AI). It's an exciting time, but it's also a period of enormous anxiety. People understand that jobs and how we work are on the line. The philanthropic sector is not immune, and neither are fundraisers.

But, while it's a time of uncertainty, we have to remain positive and optimistic that things will work out—they always do. Even if you begin to research and learn about the issues, inevitably, you adapt to the changes and move with the times. Ultimately, that places you in a much better position to experience the inevitable evolution than others.

There was a time when nonprofits hired a team of fundraisers. The team leader was a development director with a major gifts officer, an events person, and a grant writer. Today, nonprofits can do what it took the director of development and the major gifts officer a few days—or even months—in a couple of minutes.

The development team's work can also get completed at a fraction of the cost with better results. Nonprofits seek to invest in artificial intelligence. In the book from which I took the quote for the opening of this chapter, three essential ingredients allow organizations to harness AI's power for growth. In that book, the authors offer insights about how any company, and yes, even nonprofits, could take advantage of artificial intelligence's benefits through 1) scale, 2) scope, and 3) learning.

In short, technology has the power to disrupt any business or industry, for that matter, wholly. Because of the power of artificial intelligence and machine learning, organizations could grow in scale, scope, and learning beyond what they ever imagined. Scale is the growth of the work done by an organization.

In referring to scope, it means going beyond what you do to other areas because of technical abilities. And finally, learning is the knowledge coming from data and tech that informs business and nonprofit leaders. For instance, because of the power of AI to scour the entire internet and spot patterns, it could deliver results that allow managers to predict when and how to approach their customers.

The siloes that existed within companies, and nonprofits, which limits growth, are coming down. Even more fascinating is the reality that business leaders don't have to restrict themselves any longer to one particular industry.

As we know, the world experienced a pandemic in 2020. Both Pfizer, AstraZeneca, and Moderna, Johnson & Johnson, among others, came out as leaders in the production of vaccines. Typically, vaccines would take years of research, trials, and testing. However, the world experienced Pfizer, AstraZeneca, and Moderna move toward producing vaccines in less than one year. That is truly remarkable and a first for the world. It wouldn't be possible without the technology we have in the 21st Century.

Moderna: A Different Kind of Biotech Company

In the book, *Competing in the Age of AI: Strategy and Leadership When Algorithms and Networks Run the World*" by Marco Iansiti and Karim R. Lakhanti, the authors wrote about Moderna. They wrote, "*…is purpose-built for this kind of rapid response and exponential impact*" as it relates to a situation like the COVID pandemic. According to the authors, the CEO, Stéphane Bancel, says they are a technology company that does biology.

In essence, their pharmaceuticals get created by their software to determine what proteins the human body needs to produce to fight a specific disease. As Iansiti and Lakhanti explained, the company is an "AI factory," which uses data and technology in every aspect of the company. AI factories create solutions using both business intelligence, which is data-driven and no longer relies on intuitions, hunches, or even experience. It combines business intelligence with artificial intelligence.

As a result of the technological advances, we have wholly moved from the industrial age headlong into the digital age. Now companies, and nonprofits, can do what was once considered impossible. For instance, several companies created a pandemic vaccine that went from research to market in less than a year—previously undoable. However, it was possible because of the power of data, artificial intelligence, and machine learning, informing what humans wanted and needed to get done.

Artificial Intelligence in the Nonprofit Sector

In a discussion I had with Shawn about AI's future in the nonprofit sector, he stressed that human/machine team powers the most potent form of AI. He also said we are not at a fulcrum of replacing human development directors, but with AI, we can empower them to be more productive and efficient and focus on what they are good at, the art of fundraising.

As you know, I'm a fundraiser, and something professional fundraisers have said for a long time is that what we do is both an art and a science. The idea that the more AI improves and the "science" gets handled in a fraction of the time so I could focus on what I do best, which is relationship building, is attractive. I'm sure that many other fundraisers feel the same.

I appreciate Shawn's idea and thoughts that AI's strength is the human/machine team. I'm also mindful of the changes coming to the sector and the evolution of how fundraisers and other professionals within nonprofit groups work. For instance, I could easily see a world where program officers could predict when they need to increase food supplies at a food bank because of data information and AI learning from patterns.

Perhaps there's more need during the holidays or economic downturns. Still, AI has the power to spot patterns with varied data sets, say including the unemployment rate in a given community, and predict for program officers how many meals will be necessary that month. AI is redefining processes and how things get accomplished.

Through software such as boodle.AI, we now have the technology where fundraisers could get incredible predictive intelligence about opportunities for giving. boodle.AI, for instance, takes nonprofit databases and checks it against more than 500 demographic, behavioral, and other attributes belonging to 220 million American adults to offer fundraisers "intelligent fundraising." In other words, the guesswork—or the art, some would say—is getting taken out of fundraising so that fundraisers get better targets, donor scoring for prioritization and segmentation.

Going back to the Introduction and Shawn Olds' quote. *"AI fundraising platform boodleAI has helped nonprofits acquire a $1,000 new donor in 10 minutes, raise $3,600 in new donors in one hour, raise $10,000 in* *new donations in one week and achieve email donation rates 100 times the average."* It's not something that will happen. It's not in the future. It's all happening now.

boodleAI, for example, is a company in the nonprofit sector that seeks to disrupt it by making it much more efficient and powerful. And the reality is that donors and the public want this sort of efficiency. It's up to individual nonprofits and the sector as a whole to determine how they will move forward in the age of artificial intelligence. For our purposes, the best place to begin is by understanding what artificial intelligence is and how it's integrating itself into the philanthropic sector.

What is Artificial Intelligence?

To understand AI's power, you have to know a bit about what it is and how it works. In essence, artificial intelligence is intelligent computing. Meaning, today's computers are small but incredibly powerful. By definition, intelligent computing means that machines can learn—for themselves. Whereas in the past, your programmers were feeding computers information for new learning. Today's technology can learn for itself based on the knowledge and information it acquires as it accomplishes tasks.

For example, we know that millions of people spend time on social media, and billions have Facebook accounts. You've probably heard a lot about algorithms. Those algorithms are artificial intelligence. So, in the simplest terms, let's say you have 100 friends on Facebook. Every day, you get on Facebook, and you like or comment on your closest friends. In that bunch, you also have a friend or two whom you don't engage with for whatever reason when you're scrolling through your timeline.

Over time, Facebook AI *learns* that you must not be too interested in those two friends, so eventually, although they remain as Facebook friends, you won't see much of any of their future posts. In other words, Facebook's artificial intelligence learned and *predicted* you don't want to engage with those particular people.

As the years' pass, the chances are that AI will learn a lot more about us, our lives, and what we need. So, it's crucial, particularly as AI enters our homes and offices, to understand a bit about how they work. By doing so, when the time comes to hire a technology vendor for your charity, you'll appreciate a few high-level concepts.

As I described in my example about Facebook, artificial intelligence can learn your preferences and make predictions about how you will behave. The ability for artificial intelligence to learn is called "machine learning." In fact, in computer science, some programmers spend their time programming what AI needs to know independently. Therefore, the programming done by humans creates artificial intelligence that does machine learning. It is that learning that then allows AI to predict who you want to see on your Facebook feed or the films you want to see on Netflix or Hulu.

The Ethics of Artificial Intelligence

As artificial intelligence enters into every aspect of our collective existence, I think there's a critical topic for nonprofits to understand, primarily since they exist to help society—ethics. Nonprofits and social enterprises have a special responsibility for ethical behavior. Also, the public demands it, and it's why it is fast to take a group to a task that does not behave ethically.

For instance, we know of cases where human biases[8] have been introduced into algorithms for AI. Thus, we have situations where these biases have adversely affected people seeking employment and justice in the courts as an example. Therefore, while technology is awesome and we could use it, for instance, to cure diseases, we have to be mindful of the biases. As an example, it's essential to examine bias in recruiting software.

Many organizations, including small nonprofits, are jumping on the bandwagon and purchasing software for recruiting. Platforms such as SmartRecruiters or HigherMe.com allow groups to rank and score applicants for job openings. The recruiting process is convenient for both hiring managers and applicants. Managers get reporting that scores each candidate based on their resume and the job requirements and additional factors, such as the candidate's availability for work hours or the distance an applicant lives from the office (the closer the commute, the higher the score).

For the applicant, artificial intelligence can answer questions that they might have without waiting for office hours or applying by text. Also, interview scheduling can happen quickly when an employer reaches out to a candidate. The applicant selects available timeslots, for example. Gone are the days of back and forth emails or coordination calls. Still, these platforms have the potential for problems.

First, as I mentioned, you could obtain—without your knowledge—a recruiting platform that has human bias already baked into its

---

8 "Tackling bias in artificial intelligence (and in humans)," McKinsey & Company, June 2019, https://www.mckinsey.com/featured-insights/artificial-intelligence/tackling-bias-in-artificial-intelligence-and-in-humans

DNA. So, you can end up with a platform that might discriminate against gender or other variables. You can also set it and forget it and never really have human oversight over your organization's artificial intelligence. In other words, human eyes, supervision, and review on everything that artificial intelligence processes are essential.

PwC published a report[9] that addressed what organizations have to do when using artificial intelligence, and it behooves your group to realize that with artificial intelligence comes having to ensure ethical behavior. The following are essential topics that PwC reported as necessary elements of artificial intelligence:

1. *Fairness: Are we minimizing bias in our data and AI models? Are we addressing bias when we use AI?*

2. *Interpretability: Can we explain how an AI model makes decisions? Can we ensure those decisions are accurate?*

3. *Robustness and security: Can we rely on an AI system's performance? Are our AI systems vulnerable to attack?*

4. *Governance: Who is accountable for AI systems? Do we have the proper controls in place?*

5. *System ethics: Do our AI systems comply with regulations? How will they impact our employees and customers?*

Nonprofit leaders and even donors are in unique positions to push technology companies to act responsibly and ethically. And the way to have the ability to encourage vendors to ensure ethical behavior is to understand all of the issues concerning artificial intelligence. To that end, an essential argument of how we should view artificial intelligence was written in an op-ed for *The New York Times*[10] by Dr. Stuart Russell. He is a professor of computer science at the University of California, Berkeley.

There are two fundamental ideas that Dr. Russell noted in his op-ed. The first is, "The "standard model" in AI, borrowed from philosophical and economic notions of rational behavior, looks like this: *"Machines are*

---

9 "2019 AI Predictions," PwC, United States, https://www.pwc.com/us/en/services/consulting/library/artificial-intelligence-predictions-2019.html?WT.mc_id=CT3-PL300-DM1-TR1-LS4-ND30-TTA5-CN_ai2019-ai19-ggl1&eq=CT3-PL300-DM1-CN_ai2019-ai19-ggl1#section3

10 "How to Stop Superhuman AI. Before It Stops Us," Dr. Stuart Russell, The New York Times, October 8, 2019, https://www.nytimes.com/2019/10/08/opinion/artificial-intelligence.html?smid=nytcore-ios-share

*intelligent to the extent that their actions can be expected to achieve **their** objectives."* What Dr. Russell means by that is that at present, machines don't have any objectives that they determine on their own. Artificial intelligence does not achieve its own purposes—it realizes that of humans.

However, Dr. Russell argues that this approach to artificial intelligence is erroneous. If we are wrong on our objectives, and because AI is smarter than us, then we may have serious problems. As he goes on to argue, social media is an example. Programmers manipulate human preferences, and we have issues with democracy. As another example, he asks a chilling question. As Dr. Russell wrote in the op-ed, *"The effects of a super-intelligent algorithm operating on a global scale could be far more severe. What if a super-intelligent climate control system, given the job of restoring carbon dioxide concentrations to preindustrial levels, believes the solution is to reduce the human population to zero?"*

Think of how terrifying that could be for everyone on our planet. Dr. Russell also argues that "pulling the plug" might not be possible. AI might prevent that from happening (remember, it is much smarter than we are and predicts human behavior). But, before you lose all hope, there is another path that Dr. Russell offers us. He continues, *"The solution, then, is to change the way we think about AI. Instead of building machines that exist to achieve their objectives, we want a model that looks like this: 'Machines are **beneficial** to the extent that their actions can be expected to achieve **our** objectives.'"*

With that understanding, let's go back to the example of artificial intelligence and recruiting. As Dr. Russell explained, we want artificial intelligence to help us achieve our objectives, not its goals. Therefore, to ensure that we do not end up in a situation where AI does what it wants for its purposes—and not ours—nonprofit leaders have a special obligation to consider AI's ethical issues. It's not just in recruiting, but also in fundraising, operations, and programs.

Finally, on this point, I want to mention that some wealthy donors understand the challenges that humans face as we integrate it fully into all areas of our lives. It goes to my earlier point that donors drive the priorities in the nonprofit sector. Because they understand what's at stake, they're leading the path as it relates to artificial intelligence.

According to *The Chronicle of Philanthropy*,[11] nine donors have do-

---

11 "Donors Pour $583 Million Into Artificial-Intelligence Programs and Research," Maria Di Mento, The Chronicle of Philanthropy, October 15, 2018, https://www.philanthropy.com/article/Donors-Pour-583-Million-Into/244801

nated $585.5 million to nonprofits developing AI tools and studying the impact of artificial intelligence on human lives. Those individuals include the late Paul Allen, who co-founded Microsoft, Reid Hoffman, co-founder LinkedIn, and Elon Musk, co-founder of PayPal and Tesla Motors. Financier Stephen Schwarzman donated $350 million to MIT to work on "ethical applications of artificial intelligence."

Again, donors drive the discussion, and nonprofit groups can address one of the most significant issues related to artificial intelligence—ethics. Now that we've dealt with artificial intelligence's ethical use, let's focus on its power. Nothing else will change human history in ways we have yet to know, as will artificial intelligence. Sure, human history has dealt with famine, war, disease, the Renaissance, and the Industrial Revolution, for example. However, with artificial intelligence, humans have met something that supersedes our intellect and abilities for once.

How Technology is Moving to What Was Once Impossible

As I wrote this book, I came across an article in *The New York Times*.[12] The article showed how artificial intelligence creates images that look like people you could know or passed on the street or on your social timeline. All of the faces are friendly, but there's only one problem. Not a single one of the faces is a human who exists. Furthermore, you could create a computer-generated image for less than $3.

The technology is called a generative adversarial network. In the process, you feed computers pictures of real people, and then it's up to the software to create new images of "people." Imagine a world where on social media, for instance, we start to follow accounts of influencers who are fake people with fake children and—fake lives. I could see a reality where these accounts become influencers, and advertisers will show images of "people" having a grand time sipping champagne at the top of Mount Everest.

However, while you might wonder about some technology uses, there are undoubtedly many areas where tech is fantastic. For instance, we have the real-life example of vaccines getting created in record time (what took years, now only taking months) so that the world could start to inoculate people against COVID-19.

Virtual reality is another form of technology that will bring lots of new experiences to people. Imagine someone who could no longer travel

---

12 "Designed to Deceive: Do These People Look Real to You?" Kashmir Hill and Jeremy White, The New York Times, November 21, 2020, https://www.nytimes.com/interactive/2020/11/21/science/artificial-intelligence-fake-people-faces.html

or is sick in bed traveling all over the world through virtual reality programs. Augmented reality could assist young surgeons in their training and preparations. In short, technology is a truly transformative force that is unlike anything we ever experienced, and it's slipping into our day-to-day lives in many ways.

Think about your phone and our digital assistants. I have Alexa at home and prefer not having to type into my cell phone when all I want to know is if it's going to rain. All I do is ask, and it informs me how I should prepare to greet the day. In short, many of us have allowed technology to enter our lives, and it's making our lives easier. If you get lost in a new city, you don't have to walk around clueless or asking strangers. You could just pull out your phone and speak to your digital voice assistant to direct you.

Technology is permeating our lives in ways that are large and small. As we move to smart homes, in a few short years, millions will speak to their homes using voice commands to lower the thermostat in the house, turn on the stove where you placed left-overs from the evening before to warm-up, or turn on the lights before you walk in the door. Already, millions make use of that technology and others that keep their homes safe when they are away on vacation. Remember asking your neighbor to drop by your place or leaving lights on (and wasting energy)? That's no longer necessary.

However, there is a balance we have to strike as a society. The public, including consumers, businesses, and nonprofits, have to ensure that because technology, including artificial intelligence and machine learning, are so incredibly powerful, that we have a check on it somehow. Legislation has started to get created around data protection, which you will read about in Chapter Three, but the chances are we will have to go further with it. I'm not sure anyone knows what technology will look like thoroughly in 5, 10, or 20 years. One thing's for sure; it is going to be unlike anything we've seen.

Because of its immense power, as a whole, we have to enjoy the benefits of technology, but also reign it in when necessary, and always push for the ethical use of the enormous capabilities we now have at our disposal. In short, all of us have to be informed citizens and understand what it means to live as responsible citizens in a world where you *can't* always believe what you see as real.

What You See Is Only What It's Predicted You Want to See
Artificial intelligence is powerful. There's no question about it. Moreover, it could be used to accomplish many great things related to improving the

lives of people around the world. However, as with everything else in life, there could certainly be a downside to this immense power. One of the areas is social media.

Social media has torn down borders. The moment you post something in one part of the world, you could have someone on the other side of the planet responding. For nonprofits, social media has been an excellent tool because they have been able to share their stories and get supporters and donate to give to their causes for a much lower cost.

However, there's a darker side to social media, which you'll see concerning data privacy later in the book. As a global society, we also have other issues we have to deal with concerning giant social media platforms. For one, we have to concern ourselves with the threat of social media on democratic societies.

Look, I'm not a big social networking user, but I understand that AI learns what you want to see, and then it predicts what you want to see—to the exclusion of other ideas and voices. It doesn't matter what side of the political side you find yourself on. If you don't listen or read ideas and thoughts from others who have differing opinions than yours, all you do is confirm what you believe to be true. Ultimately, you have a society where people view the world through entirely different frameworks, threatening democracies. For instance, millions of people genuinely believe that elections are rigged.

There's a construct in psychology called confirmation bias. It means that people tend to filter and interpret information that confirms what they believe or value. It's not something that they may be aware of, but subconsciously, they gravitate toward information that confirms their views. Moreover, these confirmation biases are strong when we gravitate toward information on deeply emotional issues for us.

Now consider AI within social media. Let's say you're a big sports fan, and as a New Yorker, you loved the Mets. It doesn't take a long time to start seeing groups and people in your timeline related to the Mets. Ultimately, if you click on those links, you'll start seeing sponsored ads from companies selling Mets gear. Let's say the Mets play for the World Series but lose, and some betting conglomerate spreads a rumor that the Mets lost because the game was rigged.

Being such a Mets fan, you start to see posts about the game rigging, likely, not actual. Nevertheless, something profound inside of you—because you are emotionally attached to the Mets—starts to believe the Mets lost because the game was rigged. The algorithms continue to feed this content to you, and your confirmation bias only reinforces with every like and comment you make that this is the content you want to see and ultimately share.

Now take this same idea about confirmation bias, and anything could be true—or not. That's how conspiracy theories spread like wildfire. It's how bullies could spread rumors about classmates, which get promoted beyond the school, and now get views in the entire community and even the world. Unfortunately, teen suicide is increasing, and researchers are exploring a correlation between that and social media.

As you can see, when anything could be shared and spread, it's easy to see how democracies themselves could be under threat. If you happen to be a passionate supporter of a particular party or candidate, and they lose. Your social media timeline starts to show how the election got rigged or votes not counted; what do you begin to believe if that's all you see?

Organizations such as the Center for Humane Technology exist to help prevent the more shady side of technology. The nonprofit exists to call the alarm about tech addiction (there's something to be said about making sure your notifications aren't on because the human mind can't help itself look when it sees notifications). Furthermore, it's created to ensure that tech companies, the public, and governments help ensure that technology gets used to improve democracies, relationships, human well-being, and information.

As you will read throughout the book, artificial intelligence and technology are profoundly changing our lives. Moreover, the ability to immensely broaden scale and scope, the nonprofit sector, or anything else, will ever be quite the same again. Technology is now infused in everything from blockchain, impact investing in fundraising technology. As you will see in the coming chapters, all of it is dismantling traditional philanthropy seeking social good.

TWO

HOW TO BRING TECHNOLOGY INTO YOUR NONPROFIT

"Technology is nothing. What's important is that you have a faith in people, that they're basically good and smart, and if you give them tools, they'll do wonderful things with them." — Steve Jobs.

As I mentioned in the previous chapter, in the book by Marco Iansiti and Karim R. Lakhanti, leaders understand that technology now offers them ways to compete that were not possible until the 21st Century. In short, technology allows teams to grow their businesses in three ways, which are necessary to compete in the modern arena:

1. Growth of **scale** concerning what your organization does.
2. Development of **scope**, allowing businesses to expand what they do in different industries.
3. Continual **learning** because with technology, decisions don't depend on human experience, but data. Because knowledge is part of growth and expansion, the organizations that get ahead are those that instill cultures of learning.

With that in mind, in this chapter, I want to share insights on how to lead the change toward becoming a tech-centered nonprofit organization. The reality is that it's a necessity. I firmly believe that those nonprofits that evolve, adapt, and bring technology and data into their work—at the core—will succeed in the coming years. Those nonprofit groups that continue with the idea that it's business as usual will lost out on endless opportunities.

We have to consider that technology is at the base of everything we do in the modern era. How we communicate with each other, how we do our banking, how we research and get information, how we work, and even the movies we watch on Netflix all have technology and algorithms at the core.

Do you think that the list of movies you see on your Netflix account is the same as anyone in your family? It's not. Even if you live with the same people, Netflix algorithms are so good that they show you different movie titles, depending on your interests, and varying movie thumbnail images and even trailers! Everything is customized.

Moreover, corporations understand that today's consumer cares about social responsibility. In recent years, the movements we've experienced from Black Lives to Me Too, and others demonstrate that the public doesn't just want lip service. They want to see actual change. They no longer wish to wait. Because of it, you have the growth of impact investing or even blockchain that completely upends and, potentially, takes out nonprofits from the equation. In other words, platforms now exist for people to donate directly to people in need.

Regarding impact investing, you have for-profit businesses seeking solutions for social problems that measure both profits and social metrics and return on investment. How's that for disrupting philanthropy? Invest in a company, do good for society, and get a financial return. If you think that the public isn't open to those new ideas, think again, as you will see later in the book.

For decades, small community-based nonprofit groups couldn't compete against large organizations and national chapter nonprofits. However, now they can. If they are smart about technology and get a team of people who understand the incredible power of technology, continuously learn, and want to grow the scale, if not the scope of their organization, it's doable. I'll share an example of a David and Goliath situation.

For years, Amazon has been the 1,000-pound gorilla in the publishing field. As you may know, Amazon started by selling books, and then it began to publish books. Unfortunately for publishers and authors, it commoditized the book industry to such an extent that it could take more of the profits, and it all but destroyed the book industry. It certainly put lots of small independent books shops out of business as well.

Nevertheless, book lovers began to understand that Amazon was destroying the book business that they loved. The "David" in this story is an online bookstore called Bookshop.org. The company sells books from local small independent bookshops to readers. Moreover, it's attracted affiliates because its commission splits are more than twice what Amazon pays.

The Bookshop team aimed to take a bit of market share away from Amazon, and during its launch, early in 2020, more than 200 booksellers signed up as affiliates. Then you had the pandemic, and the revenue for

Bookshop took off online as articles got written about the platform, and people shared information about it on social media.

I'm here to tell you that if Bookshop.org could do it against the likes of Amazon if you want to grow your nonprofit to scale and get more fundraising dollars for more programs impacting your community, you could do it. First, we'll explore technology and fundraising, specifically, and later in this chapter, we'll look at integrating artificial intelligence into the modern 21st Century nonprofit.

AI and the Nonprofit Fundraising

How is it affecting the nonprofit sector and fundraising, specifically? At the outset of this book, I stated that donors drive the conversation on solving many of our social problems. Frankly, they give where they want to make a difference. Artificial intelligence will only make it much more pronounced, which is why you already have more than $585.5 million donated to the study and development of ethical artificial intelligence. However, I believe that amount is much more considerable when you consider the global efforts by all levels of donors.

As I was researching and writing this book, I came across a piece by Ashutosh R. Nandeshwar. I appreciate his thinking,[13] and agree about artificial intelligence and fundraising. As Nandeshwar states, and if you're a professional fundraiser, you can certainly understand, donors don't like solicitation requests. We all know that.

Nevertheless, donors who care about philanthropy do care about making an impact. Artificial intelligence will only make it easier for donors to support in ways that will truly make an impact. In other words, the annual solicitations made to donors to support a cause, with little effect, are gone.

Donors now have the opportunity to understand what organizations, and they don't have to be nonprofits, are making measurable differences. If they see what they like, that's where they will choose to put their money. I'm sure you would agree that makes sense because it's a "winning" investment.

As Nandeshwar explains, when someone is making complex decisions, the brain begins to slow. It does it so it can process information. However, artificial intelligence can handle exceedingly complex and enormous amounts of data, and it can process it quickly and efficiently. Its out-

---

13 Ways Artificial Intelligence Will Disrupt Nonprofit Fundraising, Nandeshwar.info, http://nandeshwar. info/data-science-2/ways-artificial-intelligence-will-disrupt-nonprofit-fundraising/

put to the human is the best results based on the information provided.

So, as far as fundraising is concerned, donors will have the opportunity to let AI make their philanthropic decisions—based on their interests. Also, artificial intelligence will offer donors a chance to suggest the best way to disburse money, depending on the organization's opportunities for success.

For example, what if a donor is interested in supporting a program for arts for her children and is also involved in funding an effort to rescue animals? Artificial intelligence platforms will find her the best arts program for children and animal rescue groups that, based on their data and metrics, are making a significant impact in the community. But it will go further.

Perhaps the donor has the names of the arts and animal rescue programs. What Nandeshwar suggests AI will inform donors about how much to distribute to each organization, depending on their metrics. So, if she's thinking of giving $10,000, artificial intelligence will suggest that the animal rescue group receive $7,000 because of their performance and metrics and that the arts group receives $3,000.

That is a profound shift in thinking about fundraising and how it will work going forward. What Nandeshwar suggests is that nonprofits will provide their impact and giving opportunities. Artificial intelligence will scour vast amounts of data to match a donor with the best organization, and it will rank nonprofits' offerings to donors. I would suggest that it will go beyond just the nonprofits and technology platforms. It will have the ability to rank "social good" programs, including for-profit social enterprises and corporations. Of course, that will bring much more competition to the nonprofit sector, but I think that's where we are heading.

Also, of note, what Nandeshwar and I think is on the near horizon will provide donors with customization and personalization. Just as people are now used to on-demand on their social media feeds, to video streams, to vacation activities, they'll do the same in philanthropy.

Perhaps you think, well, that's something that's coming down the line. Well, the future is now. *All* nonprofit leaders and fundraisers have to shift their practices. Today's general and major donors live in a quick-paced world. They are used to having access to anything they want to know with a few mobile keyboard taps. Your donors are used to receiving information in ways they prefer.

For instance, you have people who consume information through real-world mediums such as mail, television, or radio. You also have the vast majority of people who consume everything on demand through podcasts, videos, social media, emails, and texts. Meaning, nonprofits must meet their supporters wherever they are, and that requires a multi-platform and multi-channel approach to marketing and fundraising.

Adam Treiser, Professor Decision Sciences & Analytics, Johns Hopkins University, and the founder of Arjuna Solutions presented at a meeting[14] of the Association of Philanthropic Counsel. He is correct, based on my own experience in speaking to thousands of fundraisers and donors. We are now at a point where fundraising shifted from the donor's experience to fundraising by AI. As the global philanthropist and social entrepreneur, Wayne Elsey, Founder & CEO, Funds2Orgs, noted in an article[15] about Treiser's presentation, AI brings with it three activities for donor acquisition and retention.

1. **Dynamism:** *AI provides fundraisers with the ability to recognize and respond to specific situations.*

2. **Specificity:** *AI provides fundraisers the ability to customize fundraising down to the individual and not just a segment or population.*

3. **Efficiency:** *AI allows fundraisers to ask for support in requests specifically targeted to each donor, at scale.*

Nonprofit organizations, fundraisers, and donors exist in a whole new world, increasingly involving artificial intelligence. Again, nonprofit leaders must change with the tide. So, let's take a look at the tools currently on the market that are changing the fundraising game for nonprofit groups and how they acquire and retain donors.

Fundraising Platforms Using Artificial Intelligence

By the time this book gets published, we may have more companies entering the nonprofit market seeking to sell platforms for fundraising. Technology is changing at a mind-numbing pace, and it will never be "slow" in evolving ever again. We're past that point. We now have the emergence of 5G technology and voice and speech recognition as huge game-changers

---

14 "Artificial Intelligence that optimizes Donor Lifetime Value and Retention," Adam Treiser, January 25, 2019, https://apcinc.org/docman/open/970-treiser/file

15 "Artificial Intelligence Tools Your Nonprofit Must Explore—Now," Wayne Elsey, Nonprofit PRO, April 25, 2019, https://www.nonprofitpro.com/post/artificial-intelligence-tools-your-nonprofit-must-explore-now/

going into the next year. Five years from now, we can only imagine the capabilities of artificial intelligence.

Concerning nonprofit fundraising, which is the driving theme of this book, artificial intelligence exists to help nonprofits see past fundraisers, understand what worked, and then use that information for future fundraisers. As you'll read, AI assistants exist that can tailor messaging to prospects with customized information that resonates with them, specifically.

With that said, let's take a look at the products currently on the market and what will likely remain as robust platforms for years to come for nonprofits seeking to incorporate AI into their fundraising efforts. The reality is that nonprofits that have purchased platforms using AI have experienced increases in fundraising as high as 49 percent. In other words, artificial intelligence can be a fundraising boon for nonprofits in need of revenue for their missions.

boodle.AI

The first one that I'd like to mention is boodle.AI. For the sake of transparency, I consider the executive team at this company to be my friends. That said, they are leaders in nonprofit fundraising. boodle.AI uses an artificial intelligence assistant to ensure the quality of data and to deliver machine learning-powered predictive analytics on any prospect list an organization may have, allowing higher fundraising returns. According to the company, nonprofits that use the platform have acquired ten new donors in the first week of use. They've also received $10,000 in new gifts during the first month and increased email click-through rates by a factor of 30. In one case, the system helped an established organization find a $20,000 in their email newsletter list.

Salesforce

Salesforce has been a player in the nonprofit sector for a long time. It's one of the global leaders in constituent relationship management (CRM), and the company has various solutions depending on the type of nonprofit organization and goals. It's also incorporated artificial intelligence into its products. For instance, for small and medium-sized groups, Salesforce will help you target the right donors based on your dataset's analysis. For nonprofits that choose to go with Salesforce for their CRM, they have experienced an increase of 24 percent in donor retention, as well as a 36 percent increase in donor engagement.

Gravyty

Gravyty fuses a branch of artificial intelligence known as Natural Language Processing (NLP) to increase fundraising revenue for nonprofit groups. It also has live and on-demand support from "frontline fundraisers" with an average of ten years of experience to help nonprofit leaders. Gravyty will have AI write appeal letters instead of humans. Because of it and the fact that it can analyze the database, it can increase revenue as much as 49 percent, as it did for Cure Alzheimer's Fund, with 5 percent in donor retention. In other words, you no longer have to write emails that may get you fundraising support. Artificial intelligence will now do it for you.

Blackbaud

If you've been in the fundraising sector for a while, then you understand that Blackbaud is the 800-pound gorilla in the software market for fundraising in the nonprofit sector. And, just like newer companies, Blackbaud uses artificial intelligence to increase fundraising dollars. What's more, because they have so much of the market share—and nonprofit information, they can credibly say that they have the "world's largest philanthropic data set." Its product, Intelligence for Good, uses AI for its cloud solutions and also machine learning. It also has tools for descriptive, predictive, and prescriptive analytics.

Finally, there are other solutions that you can explore for artificial intelligence for recruiting to fundraising. What's more, you need to understand how AI is changing the nonprofit landscape. That includes all of the issues that it brings, such as ethics. While we have AI that can help us fundraisers with predictive analysis, better target and message donors, and aid board members in deciding who best to ask and how new assistants, we have to be thoughtful about integrating these powerful tools into our sector. Yes, fundraising dollars may come a lot easier, but it will likely mean we will need fewer people on fundraising teams. Indeed, nonprofits will seek to recruit people with different skill sets—perhaps people with robust technology and relationship building skills—but we must keep an eye on biases that can adversely affect whole segments of people.

How to Integrate Artificial Intelligence into Your Nonprofit

As a nonprofit leader, you want to figure out how to integrate artificial intelligence into your organization. However, you have to first get your mind around how it could help your nonprofit, and then you have to become a tech-centered nonprofit, and that takes a shift in thinking. First, let's tackle the idea of what artificial intelligence could do for your nonprofit.

As we learned earlier in this chapter, AI has enormous power, and with its predictive capacity, it can ensure your fundraisers solicit your best donors, at the right time, with the right message. Candidly, AI takes a lot of the guesswork out of fundraising. In the old days, we would ask donors to support a cause based on the time of year they gave. However, AI is now powerful enough to spot patterns no human could ever see and determine precisely when you have to ask a particular donor, and the message that will resonate with them.

Another crucial thing about AI is personalization. As a fundraiser, we've been talking about customization for years, but now each donor could receive a wholly personalized email. Customization is at the core of everything. Let's take a look at Google. When you search in Google, Google predicts what you want to see based on your past searches.

I'll give you an example. A few of my colleagues tested it out recently to see how customized and personalized the results were for searching the term "climate change." We all searched for "climate change," but the results for me were about predictions, trends, and facts because Google knows that I'm usually looking for that type of information. However, the search results for a friend related to jobs because they sought work in that industry. In short, technology is predicting what we want to see, and it's delivering it to us.

Artificial intelligence is also maximizing productivity. Repetitive tasks are eliminated from human jobs as bots take over the ordinary and allow humans to deal with more critical work. Let's take chatbots, for example. Many small businesses and nonprofits use chatbots because they are adequate to answer basic questions that often get repeated. For example, let's say that you run a food bank, and you have donors who continually want to deliver food items and clothing. Chatbots could now answer on social media or your site the hours your open, the times you accept food and clothing, and the process for how you accept donations.

AI could also provide data information and research beyond what we imagined less than a decade ago. Often, fundraisers look to prioritize their donor prospects through donor screening. That's become much more sophisticated taking names and using hundreds of data points because of the digital tracks everyone leaves in everything they do digitally. What that means for nonprofits and fundraisers is that they're getting much more informed information about people when they do a wealth or donor screening.

An excellent example of what is possible now is with the Chinese company, Ant Financial, a goliath and one of the most highly valued financial tech companies globally. It is a massive company that is a digital payment platform. It also provides loans (without any human bank officers' input), is a credit rating system, offers wealth management, and offers a face recognition payment system, among its massive ecosystem of products and services. As you could see, it's a company that is massive both in scale and scope (operating across traditional industries).

Its data for learning and assessments of credit risks for loans is informed using the digital records from utility payments, purchasing patterns, transaction details from its affiliate company, and Alibaba, which is as massive as Amazon. It also gets data from a host of other public records available and screened by its artificial intelligence. In short, anything that you have ever done, digitally, in any way (e.g., sending a payment to a friend, making a purchase, sharing on social) is now fair game for companies to use. AI provides those who seek it, including nonprofits, information for smarter and more informed decisions.

The Mindshift and Process for Integrating Artificial Intelligence

I think it's fair to say that if you could think it, there's an artificial intelligence that could produce what you need. If you want to curate content, there's AI that could curate articles for you, so your marketing team doesn't have to spend hours doing it. If you want to promote your cause, AI shares your information with the best audience. If you're going to rank candidates for a job opening you have available, AI could do that and present you with a list at the press of a button with the best persons on paper in priority order. It does seem as if whatever you want, AI could do it for you.

Nonprofit leaders must take notice of what's happening. Sometimes I enjoy scrolling through social media groups, and I do a lot of reading from traditional philanthropic thought leaders. Candidly, it makes me chuckle when I see things that seem as if we were still operating in 1995. While we're reading through the umpteenth article about how to get nonprofit boards to fundraise (not necessary in the digital world), corporations and savvy business leaders embracing technology are looking to make money and do social good at the same time. All of it is possible because of technology.

So, before anything moving to a technology-centered organization, you have to have that mindset. We have all heard this ad nauseam, but to become a tech-centered nonprofit informed by data, the entire leadership team has to get on board. For starters, technology allows for the siloes within an organization to get knocked down. Therefore, your tech team's role is no longer to hoard the data.

Their job becomes much more sophisticated by allowing everyone to use technology and see the data. However, their part is about making sure that all of the technology you use integrates well with other ecosystem platforms. It's maintained, secured, and updated, and that people continually sharpen their skills because technology is always changing. No sooner have you mastered one system than it's time for the next update.

With siloes coming to an end, you could have smaller teams work together on different projects. For example, to grow your work scope, you could have a data analyst, program officer, marketing, and fundraising expert work on one program within your nonprofit. You could then replicate another team of interdisciplinary experts working on another program that grows the scope of the work you do in your community.

A model that works well for operating from a tech-centered approach to scale your operations is the hub and spoke model.[16] It's a model for distributing, in the case of nonprofits, services instead of products. As alluded to in the previous paragraph, you could set up your nonprofit to operate with an entirely different model.

All distribution of those services (i.e., spokes) gets channeled out from the hub from a small hub group. In other words, nonprofit leaders have to evaluate traditional ways of operating. They then have to decide if, with the integration of powerful technology if that is the approach that serves their interests or if they are better served by operating in new ways that are much more efficient with technology and data information at the core.

From a leadership perspective, the most fundamental idea you have to remember that experience does *not* matter in the digital world. It doesn't. Let's say you've been a nonprofit leader for a decade and believe that your program is great and optimized. However, one day, you get a new program officer, a junior person but tech-savvy. A few months after starting the job, that person brings you data and information showing you that if you offered your services during these hours (instead of the hours where you do) and in these zip codes (instead of the ones where you focus), you would be able to triple the people you serve.

---

16 "Building the AI-Powered Organization," Tim Fountaine, Brian McCarthy, Tamim Saleh, Harvard Business Review, July-August 2019, Issue, https://hbr.org/2019/07/building-the-ai-powered-organization

Does your experience tell you should continue on your path, or is that confirmation bias, discussed earlier in the book? The data suggests something entirely different. As a leader, what do you do? Do you trust your experience and gut, or do you trust the numbers and data? If you said you trust the data, that's the right answer. Still, even though it's the right answer, it's not easy. That's where the mind shift comes into play.

As a nonprofit leader, you have to lean in and trust the data and information, even when it goes against your experience and what you may believe to be accurate. Also, as a leader, you have to encourage your leadership team to do the same. Bringing in artificial intelligence and technology into any business could be scary. People don't understand it. While they're impressed with its powers and abilities, they may be more concerned with their jobs. So, it's your job to be the champion of technology, help people get comfortable with it, and support that adaptation as jobs evolve and change.

Another critical aspect of bringing technology into the core of how your nonprofit operates is to create a culture of learning. Again, technology is evolving exponentially daily. Think of when you had a smartphone and when they just came out. Apps and the operating system would get updated every once in a while. However, now, apps and operating systems are continually getting updated. If you purchase software for your nonprofit, the chances are you'll go through several updates in a given year. Why?

As technology evolves exponentially, security features need updates. As users inform and interact with the systems in varying ways, technology companies learn and make adjustments to better suit consumers' needs. In short, technology necessitates a culture of learning in your nonprofit. Everyone on your team—including those who haven't been in a classroom in decades—must update their skills and learn the technology platforms that allow you to grow your nonprofit to scale and be smart about how and when you do, for instance, fundraising campaigns.

In many ways, it's almost a good idea to think of it as Moderna does, as discussed earlier in the book. It considers itself a technology company that happens to do biology. Could you see your nonprofit organization as a technology company that happens to do social services, education, youth development, etc.? My instinct is that this idea is anathema to many nonprofit leaders because they would see it as negating their mission and the people they serve.

However, that doesn't have to be the case. You could still carry out your mission to serve those affected with cancer or in need of after-school programs. However, by thinking about integrating the power of technology into your nonprofit, you have a chance to come up with solutions that may not have been possible in the past. Repetitive tasks are a thing of the past. Information comes front and center into your decision-making, not experience and gut instincts.

Another critical mind shift that has to happen, particularly within the nonprofit sector, is to let go of the fear of failure and risk. Let's face it; the philanthropic industry could be timid in trying out ideas. In some instances, nonprofit leaders fear that they won't get donor funding if they "fail" at a project. Yet, failure and risk are part of having a tech-centered organization. Testing new ideas, platforms, processes, and projects are part of success. As the adage goes in Silicon Valley, fail fast, and fail often. Why? Because every time you fail, you learn. The more you know, the better informed you become and the better your services become.

If you want to become a tech-centered and enabled nonprofit that seeks to scale your operations, you also have to invest in technology. Fortunately, you could get a lot of technological tools that are subscription-based for a couple of hundred dollars a month, depending on the platform. Nonprofit leaders could be notoriously cheap and wanting to keep expenses down, so their operating costs are low. However, this is not how you need to be thinking to scale your nonprofit.

Instead, I would look to connect with leaders who could invest in the technology that you research to ensure you grow and provide even more services in your community, affecting more people's lives. Before you could convince others that becoming a tech and AI centered nonprofit is the way to go, you have to first immerse yourself in educating yourself on everything about technology, artificial intelligence, and machine learning. The reality is that anyone could learn it conceptually, and you don't have to be a "techie" to understand its power. Once you know it and how it could fundamentally change your nonprofit's work and grow your nonprofit, you then have to convey that information to others and inspire them with the vision of what you want to see.

You must remember that speed and flexibility are essential attributes for your organization in this brave new world. Essentially, because of the power of technology, you could achieve things that took days, if not months, to do. That's no longer the case with AI powerful enough to scan your database, everything you do, and compare it to patterns in the entire internet so it could deliver you results in mere seconds.

Everything within your organization is up for change, and I mean everything from how you do your financial reporting to your marketing, fundraising, and programmatic efforts. In short, everything could get measured and optimized with technology that's much faster and flexible than what you have in your nonprofit at this point.

Finally, everyone on your team has to be on board. Not only does everyone have to want to participate in an environment that extolls a culture of learning, but everyone has to participate and like to learn. You need people on your team who are curious, open to change, adaptable, have high emotional intelligence, are not afraid about transparency as what they do gets measured, and who are wholly on board with your new vision. In short, you're probably changing the culture of your organization, and you're asking your team to step into the future with you. They have to embrace technology and become fluent in it.

Likely, new policies (especially around data privacy) have to get developed, and your team will have to bring different skills and habits for working to the table. For instance, in 2020, we saw millions working remotely. Success as a team member in a remote environment is different from in the real world where a manager could monitor in person the work and a worker isn't distracted by children or other home influences.

How you recruit, develop, train, and manage your tech-centered nonprofit team is going to be vastly different than in the past. Ultimately, you want them invested wholly and engaged with your nonprofit as it seeks to adapt to what AI offers and scale its work and mission, and perhaps even diversify its scope of work. Imagine being a foodbank that now has the power to also support job training and education initiatives for a more holistic approach to poverty, for example.

In sum, artificial intelligence is a game-changer. As a nonprofit leader, you want to ask yourself if you're ready for everything you could start doing right now, not 2, 5, or 10 years from now—but right now. It's an exciting time for nonprofit leaders, but I'm convinced we could make profound—and good—societal change despite the uncertainty. Our industry is full of good-hearted people with the right intentions. Now, we have abilities that could make the world that we imagined a reality where diseases are eradicated, children are well-educated, and economic justice comes to all and not a few.

THREE

IS PRIVACY FOR EVERYONE, INCLUDING DONORS, DEAD?

"I'm increasingly inclined to think that there should be some regulatory oversight, maybe at the national and international level, just to make sure that we don't do something very foolish. I mean with artificial intelligence we're summoning the demon." — Elon Musk

We do not know the full power of artificial intelligence yet. Further, I don't think we fully understand what the future holds for us concerning AI. I think this is fair to say we have leading minds on both sides of the issue. For instance, people such as Stephen Hawking, Elon Musk, and others suggest we enter into a doomsday scenario.

Nick Bilton, a tech columnist for *The New York Times*, wrote that we could find ourselves in a situation where a medical AI that is programmed to eliminate cancer decides that the way to do it is by exterminating humans who are prone to the disease. There are others, such as Shawn Olds and Andrew Ng, who believe in the benefits of human and artificial intelligence partnership.

Candidly, I'm not an expert in artificial intelligence and what it could bring to humanity. I'm not sure even the global scientists, engineers, and futurists have a full sense of where we're heading with AI. Nevertheless, all of us who live on this planet have to deal with whatever is to come. Because artificial intelligence is so powerful, and we know that it will outstrip the most intelligent human's capacity to process information, we would be foolhardy not to try to understand the topics that affect us.

One of the issues brought to the fore with artificial intelligence is privacy. In this chapter, we explore the drive to increased privacy after a period where it seemed that privacy was dead. Such was the sentiment in 2010 of tech CEOs such as Facebook's Mark Zuckerberg, Google's Eric Schmidt, and Sun Microsystem's Scott McNealy. However, today, we have Zuckerberg discussing a privacy-focused future on Facebook.

So, what changed? The answer is a lot, including bots and tech, that stole personal information and misinformation campaigns. As a fundraiser, I understand all of these matters impact nonprofits, and the trend is leaning—hard—toward privacy.

Technology Goes Mainstream

As I mentioned, there was a time when the top tech CEOs were claiming that privacy was finished. Remember, communication and sharing platforms such as Facebook have only been with us for a little over a decade and a half. Facebook, which is the dominant social networking platform globally with 2.4 billion users, was founded in 2004. At the time, Mark Zuckerberg was at Harvard University, and he developed it with his fellow students and friends, Eduardo Saverin, Andrew McCollum, Dustin Moskovitz, and Chris Hughes.

Google, which is the most-used search engine globally, was founded in 1998 by Larry Page and Sergey Brin while both were Ph.D. students at Stanford University. The origins of what became Google began as a research project. At the time, search engines, which were not widely used, provided results based on how many times a search term appeared on a page.

However, Page and Brin believed that they could create a better system to rank the relationships between websites. They developed programming that offered results based on the number of pages of the site and also the number of backlinks to the site, which meant it was an authority in its subject.

The new system was initially called BackRub because of the backlinking. Thankfully, they changed the name to Google. In the early 2000s, Google gained broader traction and then took off to become what it is today as it became accessible to people beyond government and businesses. Simultaneously, personal computing hardware grew from what it was in the few millions in the early 1980s to become a genuinely mass-market product as many more millions of families brought computers into their homes. During the decades of the 1980s and 1990s that technology began to integrate into people's lives. In the early 2000s, companies such as Google and Facebook, communication, and sharing in the digital world took off, connecting people around the planet with each other.

Looking back at the early years of platforms such as Facebook, Google, and email communications, many people were excited. They had at the tips of their fingers, vast amounts of information and knowledge, so they no longer had to travel to libraries to obtain research and have access to information. Everything from news to shopping to their friends and influencers was accessible to them online.

People and businesses could communicate quickly, efficiently, and at a much lower cost than in the past with travel, print, and mail. As exciting as those early years were, inevitably, there were unforeseen events that happened as the world became almost entirely digitized. It was only a matter of time when privacy would be a concept we would have to defend, and today, that's where we are as a society.

21st Century Data Breaches

To understand where we are, including fundraisers and nonprofits, with having to protect data, we have to take a look at what happened in souring the public on the idea that privacy was dead. The 21st Century seems to be full of data breaches on everything from banking information to sensitive passwords and social media accounts. This steady drip of violations on the personal information of tens or hundreds of millions, or even billions of people, has created the impetus for governments and companies (hello Apple) to pay attention to data protection. The public demands it, and because of it, governments are responding.

Explaining what occurred with a few of the most massive data hacks of the 21st Century[17] could be a book in and of itself. Therefore, for this book, we'll only explore a few of the most notorious hacks that I think soured the public on the idea that their data and personal information were no longer theirs.

Again, understanding these events helps nonprofit leaders understand that privacy is essential for the public and donors. Furthermore, suppose nonprofits do not know how a data breach at their organization could lead not only to angry donors but also liability and the end of their charity. In that case, they probably should not be in operation anyway.

Yahoo

The most significant data breach, so far, affected 3 billion users around the world and happened in 2013 and 2014. When this came to light, Yahoo was in the midst of negotiations to sell the company to Verizon. Instead, during a sensitive time, Yahoo found itself publicly announcing that it had

---

17 "The 18 biggest data breaches of the 21st century," Taylor Amerding, CSO, https://www.csoonline.com/article/2130877/the-biggest-data-breaches-of-the-21st-century.html

been hacked—the largest in history—by a "state-sponsored actor."

The information stolen included names, birthdays, telephone numbers, emails, and passwords for its users. Ultimately, that admission, which started with the company admitting 500 million users affected, was followed by another stating that 1 billion people were affected to 3 billion. It sold for $350 million lower because of the initial admission.

Equifax

As most adults in the United States know, Equifax is one of the largest three credit bureaus. It is a company that has the data of millions of people and reports on their creditworthiness. Because personal background checks in the US often include credit checks, the information it holds is highly sensitive and impacts millions' job prospects.

So, it was disturbing for the public to learn in 2017 that the company got hacked and their information compromised. Thieves stole personal data from Equifax, including birthdates, addresses, drivers' license numbers, and Social Security numbers from 143 million people. Also, 290,000 people had their credit card information exposed.

Ashley Madison

In July 2014, the world experienced a different kind of hack that shocked and caused a massive global debate about privacy. In this case, a group that called itself "The Impact Team" hacked and stole the data of users on the Ashley Madison site. Ashley Madison was a website used by people who purportedly wanted to have extramarital affairs.

What made this hack so shocking and electric in the public consciousness is that The Impact Team threatened to expose Ashley Madison users' names. These people were presumably having extramarital affairs, and the hackers said if the company did not shut itself down, the clients would get exposed.

Ashley Madison had a policy of not deleting any user information, including real names, addresses, credit card information, and other information. People who were users of the platform and who presumably did not want their spouses, colleagues, friends, or families to find out about their affairs dreaded the exposure of their information and any public shaming that would follow. Unfortunately, some people killed themselves, including a pastor and professor at New Orleans Baptist Theological Seminary.

While this caught the public's collective imaginations, millions of people who did not use Ashley Madison and its users said that users had a right to privacy. The world debated the ethics, morality, and issues of confidentiality around this particular hack. It was one of the hacks that demonstrated to the world that anyone could get hacked. No information was private, and essentially, this could happen to anyone concerning anything.

Facebook Cambridge Analytica

In early 2018, the news exploded with what became known as the Facebook Cambridge Analytica political scandal. Cambridge Analytica harvested the personal information and profiles of as many as 87 million people who used Facebook without their consent or knowledge. That information got used for political advertising.

Consequently, it was this harvesting of their data that genuinely frustrated and angered the public. The scandal is viewed as the catalyst moving the public toward the idea of a right to their data, its protection, and knowledge of how it is used.

When *The Guardian* exposed this event, Facebook did not comment on how millions of users had their information harvested for political purposes by a third party, Cambridge Analytica, without their knowledge. In the meantime, Facebook's stock price fell (it lost over $100 billion in market capital), and people spoke of the need to regulate the tech industry. In the minds of many, tech companies had too much power and, for the most part, have become massive corporations with little, if any, regulation or government oversight.

As much as Facebook declined to comment, in March of 2018, a whistleblower who worked at Cambridge Analytica by the name of Christopher Wylie came forward publicly. By the 1st of May, 2018, Cambridge Analytica closed its doors. However, by this point, the public understood how faceless technology companies—practically—owned everything about them.

Private companies had everything they needed to advertise or make money off through data mining. It includes names, addresses, credit cards, Social Security numbers, emails, credit history, work history, names of friends and other relationships, preferences for everything from movies to what they search for on the internet, etc. Perhaps privacy is dead. Nevertheless, companies and governments seek to contain some of the adverse effects of existing in a digital world.

General Data Protection Regulation

In May of 2018, the European Union law called that General Data Protection Regulation (GDPR) came into effect. It is the world's first attempt at regulating and protecting data. It is important here to say that you would be incorrect if you think your nonprofit is not affected by Europe's law. The GDPR intends to protect any digital information of people who are European citizens or residents.

However, the reach of the GDPR is global. Meaning, if you happen to have information on your donor base of people who live in one of the European Union countries, you need to make sure that you are not placing your group at significant risk. People who live in countries within the European Union have the "right to be forgotten." What that means is that if your nonprofit or any entity for that matter has information about them, you have to wipe it out—completely—if they request it from you. Notably, if you do not take care in protecting their data, you can be held liable.

Noncompliance with the GDPR, anywhere in the world, can mean a fine of as much as 4 percent of the total annual revenue. In other words, safeguarding donor data is something that all nonprofit leaders should do from a moral, ethical standing, and on principle. But, not doing it can also bring stiff penalties.

At this point, I think it's important to remind you that you may have in your database the information of people who live in Europe, and you might not even realize it. As you know, we live in a globalized world. That means that people can see information about you, through your website or social media, from anywhere.

Don't be surprised if you have one, two, or a few people who reside within the European Union. Donors and people interested in a particular cause are not limited to the country's borders where they live because of the internet and social media. So, always, always protect the information you have in your database in response to far-reaching laws. It includes the GDPR and other laws inside the US, which now exists, with more to come in the years ahead.

The GDPR information you must protect includes names, addresses, telephone numbers, emails, Social Security numbers, messages back and forth, and even IP addresses.

Privacy and Data Protection Regulation in the USA

Lest you think that data protection and privacy regulations and laws are only happening in some other country or the European Union, you need to pay attention to the United States. California became the first state in the nation to have a law go into effect concerning privacy.

In January of 2020, the Consumer Privacy Act became law in California, and it is considered the "GDPR lite." In other words, it looks a lot like the GDPR, but the penalties for violations are a lot less. Consumers, or donors, can sue the company or nonprofit for $750 per violation. Further, the State of California can penalize the organization for up to $7,500 for each penalty. While this is not 4 percent of the total annual revenue, if a nonprofit gets charged with violating this law, these penalties can still be significant.

In August 2018, I wrote an article, *"Donor Data Is at Risk in the Nonprofit Sector: What Can Be Done?"* in *Nonprofit Pro* that bears repeating in this book, and specifically in this chapter. The US Constitution enshrines privacy into law. Meaning, privacy is not a new concept and is something that our Founding Fathers thought about judiciously as they drafted and then signed the Constitution and the Bill of Rights. As I noted in the article,

> *The reality is that we all have a right to privacy in the United States, even if it is not expressly stated in the Constitution. However, the Bill of Rights does protect privacy in the 1st Amendment concerning religion, the 3rd Amendment regarding the home, the 4th Amendment related to unreasonable searches, and the 5th Amendment concerning the right to protect oneself against self-incrimination. Today, our leaders and politicians continue to try to guide the nation in that spirit, especially when their constituents, to whom they are beholden, become more vocal about the issue. It's fair to say that the public is tired of having their private information compromised, exposed, or shared, even if it is with regulators.*

California may be the first state in the nation to create a "GDPR lite" law to protect privacy, but it certainly will not be the last. Other states, such as Nevada, Washington, New Jersey, and New York, have also moved to protect data privacy, and others are expected to follow. As an example of what states are considering, New York introduced a bill that would allow New York State residents to sue companies if their data protection is violated and they suffer injury.

Privacy has become a fresh idea once again. Concurrently, companies such as Apple have positioned their brands around the concept. As a result, Apple states that privacy is a human right. Thus, it has positioned privacy as a competitive advantage over other companies in its products' marketing. They're betting that privacy makes good business sense, but it doesn't end there. It also makes good sense to earn more profits.

Using Nonprofits for Fraud & Prevention

Nonprofits have highly sensitive information about their donors. It would be a mistake to think that they are exempt from protecting that data. Not doing so can be costly in many ways. MobileCause, which provides online and event software, has an excellent approach to safeguard donors' information.

In their nonprofit security page,[18] they offer some tips that nonprofits have to be aware of for their groups. By the way, they also note—correctly—that smaller nonprofits are prime targets for hackers because they lack the resources to understand and execute comprehensive security efforts. However, even the smallest nonprofits cannot ignore protecting donor information. As a lawyer, I can tell you that those who don't secure data run a risk of losing their nonprofit status because of the bad press and regulations.

As is explained in the MobileCause security page, "card testing" increased by 200 percent in 2017. Card testing is a fraudulent activity. Hackers test stolen card numbers and see if the cards remain valid. It is done with automation that attempts to make donations to nonprofits for small amounts. If the charge goes through, hackers get alerted that the card is active, and they then move to charge higher costs. As a result, nonprofits are a testing ground for hackers and fraud with credit cards. Hackers like doing this testing through nonprofits because they often lack the controls to pick up on fraudulent activities.

MobileCause's security page notes that every nonprofit should ensure the following through its platforms:

- Certified PCI DSS Level 1, which are global security standards.
- Encryption.
- Fraud protection against card testing and other criminal activities.
- Banking and credit card security.
- Two factor-authentication for passwords.

18 Nonprofit Data Security, MobileCause, https://www.mobilecause.com/nonprofit-data-security/

MobileCause is, of course, just one of the platforms providing nonprofits with privacy and security. There are others, but the National Council of Nonprofits offers an excellent source for more information on data and security. They have plenty of resources that I would suggest you take a look at concerning cybersecurity[19].

Forthcoming Databox Revolution

Now that you have a high-level understanding of data and security, I think it's important to talk about a revolutionary idea. Imagine a way for you and your donors to control all of your online data. It exists already, and I predict that it will be something that will become mainstream—including with donor data—in the not too distant future.

A databox holds the personal information of a person. It is one way that technology companies are creating solutions to protect consumers who are demanding protection. When you place your data into a data box, you control it. Then, you provide third-parties with access to the information that you want them to have about you. Only authorized third parties will receive information from individuals through databox platforms.

As explained in an article in the BBC,[20] the idea for the databox originated in a school of thought called "Human Data Interaction (HDI)." Meaning, that personal information gets viewed as an object in its own right, rather than a derivative of technology. In other words, data is considered an asset in this school of thought or even a currency or commodity. The idea for a databox stems from the "crisis of trust" that exists in the current environment. And in response, it allows individuals to take full control of their information and, through approved applications and platforms, share the information with others when and how they want.

As the same article explains, the following are the three underlying principles for the idea of a databox:

> 1. ***Legibility*** *recognizes that data flows and data processes are often opaque to individuals and are therefore concerned to make data and data processing, including algorithmic operations, transparent and comprehensible, or accountable to users.*

---

19 Cybersecurity for Nonprofits, National Council of Nonprofits, https://www.councilofnonprofits.org/tools-resources/cybersecurity-nonprofits

20 Research, and Development, BBC, https://www.bbc.co.uk/rd/projects/databox

2. **Agency** *recognizes the need to empower people to manage their data and third-party access. This includes the ability to opt-in or opt-out of data processing and the broader ability to engage with data collection, storage, and use and understand and modify data and the inferences drawn from it.*

3. **Negotiability** *recognizes that data processing is essentially a social act involving not only computers but also human actors. This includes organizations as well as individuals and requires that people be able to manage the social interactions implicated in data processing and that they can derive value from data processing operations for themselves.*

At present, we all operate in a cloud-based world. As a result, that means that all of our digital interactions go somewhere—up into the so-called "cloud." We then trust that our information is kept safe and protected. It's incredible to think about how much data we give away on any given day.

For instance, we input our Social Security numbers, names, emails, addresses, dates of birth, and a whole host of other information into websites and other platforms. Then we trust that a third-party will be ethical and have the resources to protect our most sensitive information. We share our pictures on social media and social networking sites, those of our children, photos of our homes, vacations, purchases we've made, or places where we've donated. All of this is a dream for marketers as the data becomes mega-data, parsed, and analyzed to receive more marketing and advertising so that information can be sold to yet other third-parties for more commerce.

All the while, we have zero ability to control our data, except for not participating in a digital world, which is not practical for most of us. All we can do is trust that nothing happens that will hurt us in any way. The public understands that their information is vulnerable—even in the corporations that should have the resources to have the latest in security. So, the idea of a databox, which moves our personal information off third-party platforms back into our control to some extent, is appealing to the public and will become more so as people understand their security options.

Databoxes allow for people to hold their private information in their personal ecosystems. Incidentally, as the idea of databoxes grows, people will have greater control of the information they share when corporations, businesses, and yes, nonprofits can only obtain encrypted code or information about individuals. Again, this is a revolution in the making, but I believe millions of people think it is way overdue. Yet, at this point, you might be wondering, what does that mean for my nonprofit? Why should I care?

There are several reasons why the idea of databoxes will affect your organization. For starters, the notion of privacy will again ingrain itself in the collective consciousness of people. For many years, the public was conditioned to give and share their most sensitive information freely. Transparency is a word that you hear repeatedly, and a lot of it comes from technology companies, for example, which are not transparent. If they were, we might understand how their algorithms work and how they encourage our behaviors to keep surrendering information.

However, as consumers become used to more data protection with databoxes and other technology created to protect the information, they will expect it from nonprofits. Thus, organizations that do not adhere to data standards stand to lose fundraising dollars. Let me ask you the following question.

As databoxes and other platforms for security and privacy become more mainstream and ubiquitous, and more companies and nonprofits sign-on so they can retain business and fundraising dollars, do you think donors will give to those groups that don't adhere to basic privacy and data protection standards? I would say that the chances are high that donors and the public won't do business or donate to nonprofits that don't care enough about their data to protect it.

Let's take it one step further. Let's assume that the idea of data boxes and privacy technology gets well-incorporated into society, just as social media has done for about a decade. Finally, let's assume, all of the data sold back and forth, including nonprofits for acquisitions or donor profiling, gets harder to come by. What happens to the fundraisers?

We know from the first chapter that artificial intelligence is a game-changer. What happens when privacy and data protection become the norm and not just the competitive advantage for organizations? What happens with the information that fundraisers, especially major gift officers, seek to obtain so they know how and when to cultivate and make asks of donors?

Again, we'll find ourselves in a situation—in short order—where tech-savvy donors and prospects push nonprofits to adhere to their standards. Wealthy donors may be the first to protect much of their personal information in databoxes. However, so will people such as Generation X, who was raised understanding and appreciating privacy.

Of course, younger generations may also do the same. As an example, they already seek to find private platforms, such as Telegram or Signal, for communication. Because they share information on social media, don't assume that Millennials and Generation Z do not appreciate privacy and data security.

How things will unwind is not yet answered. Unfortunately, I don't have all the answers to all of the questions around technology and how it will impact us. As I've mentioned, I'm a lawyer and fundraiser by training, not a fortuneteller with a crystal ball or a genius futurist. However, I'm already thinking about these things. I'm speaking to thought leaders in technology in the nonprofit and law sectors, trying to understand what is just over the horizon.

Things are moving fast, blazing fast in many cases, and it's all because of technology. Everyone, especially marketers and fundraisers in the nonprofit sector, has to pay attention and look ahead. With the snap of a finger, it seems that tomorrow becomes today. Things we did not think possible only a few years ago are already a reality, and we know that the rate of growth of technology is exponential. All of this, as well as the hacks, is fueling the desire to return to some form of privacy.

For the time being, as a nonprofit leader and fundraiser, you should understand the current regulations, such as the GDPR and the news ones in California, New York, Nevada, New Jersey, and Washington. Look at the information and data you have, and think about how to secure and protect it. Ask a major donor to help you with that effort if you don't have the financial means to ensure you have the highest protection standards for the digital information you keep. Also, keep an eye on the evolution of technology, such as with data boxes and other tools that will change the landscape of how organizations gather and process data they receive from their constituents.

FOUR

THE IMPACT OF DONOR-ADVISED FUNDS

"I've learned that you shouldn't go through life with a catcher's mitt on both hands. You need to be able to throw something back."
— *Maya Angelou*

The first donor-advised fund was created in 1931 by the New York Community Foundation. Even though it's nearly 100 years since the first fund, today, donor-advised funds affect how fundraisers develop their strategic development plans. Therefore, it is essential first to understand what a donor-advised fund is, commonly referred to as a DAF. Even if you lead a small nonprofit, you may already have received a gift from a donor-advised fund.

At its core, when a donor creates a DAF, the donor makes a tax-deductible gift in the year the donation gets made. Technically, the assets become owned by the DAF sponsoring organization, such as Fidelity, Schwab, or other institutions. These groups manage and invest the money from the DAFs to make more money.

Whenever the donor chooses, be it the year the donation gets made or later years, charitable contributions get made on the recommendation and on behalf of the donor who created the account. That said, an essential element for every fundraiser to understand is the following. A donor does not need to make a gift in any year once the funds go into the DAF. However, in some sponsoring organizations, such as Fidelity, a donor must make a gift of $50 every three years to a charitable cause.[21]

The assets are controlled by a nonprofit called the sponsoring organization. In other words, financial powerhouses such as Fidelity have created charitable institutions so they can accept philanthropic funds. Be-

21 "5 Things to Know About Donor-Advised Funds," Penelope Wang, Consumer Reports, December 7, 2019, https://www.consumerreports.org/charitable-donations/donor-advised-funds-things-to-know/

cause sponsoring organizations have these nonprofit arms, they can accept charitable donations, and the donor gets a tax deduction.

The sponsoring organization invests the assets and manages the donor's account. Community foundations and nonprofit arms of financial service firms such as Schwab and Fidelity serve as sponsoring organizations. In short, there and varying ways to where sponsoring organizations exist. For instance, community trusts also handle these sorts of funds, such as the National Philanthropic Trust. In fact, DAFs were conceived by community foundations decades ago to serve donors better and the communities in which they live.

America's ten biggest sponsors of donor-advised funds took in $37.1 billion in 2018, which was up 24 percent from 2017, according to *The Chronicle of Philanthropy*.[22] As you would imagine, donor-advised funds continue to grow at a rapid pace, according to the annual analysis by the National Philanthropic Trust. Total assets under management in donor-advised funds were $121.4 billion in 2018.

Grants from donor-advised funds rose to $23.4 billion in 2018; however, the payout rate declined to 20.9 percent of total assets in 2018. Nevertheless, the number of donor-advised fund accounts jumped in 2018 to 728,560, with much of the growth attributed to small donor-advised funds.

Some of the new funds' money is going to use in new ways, such as through the creation of vehicles for employee giving programs. The average size of a donor-advised fund has dropped from about $238,860 to $166,650.[23] This could indicate that more people with lower income levels realize the benefits of donor-advised funds and create DAFs for themselves, their families, and legacies. Further, according to an article in *Nonprofit Quarterly*,[24]

> *The facts are that there are over $121 billion in DAF accounts, and over $23 billion in new contributions from*

---

22 "10 Largest Donor-Advised Funds Grew Sharply in 2018," Michael Theis, The Chronicle of Philanthropy, December 10, 2019, https://www.philanthropy.com/article/10-Largest-Donor-Advised-Funds/247685

23 "Contributions to Donor-Advised Funds Up 20 Percent in 2018," Michael Theis, The Chronicle of Philanthropy, November 12, 2019, https://www.philanthropy.com/article/Contributions-to-Donor-Advised/247518

24 "Where Have All the Donors Gone? The Continued Decline of the Small Donor and the Growth of Megadonors," Patrick M. Rooney, Nonprofit Quarterly, December 4, 2019, https://nonprofitquarterly.org/where-have-all-the-donors-gone-the-continued-decline-of-the-small-donor-and-the-growth-of-megadonors/

DAF accounts were given in 2018 (see Table 5). Grants made to charities from DAF accounts totaled the equivalent amount of 12.7 percent of total household giving in 2018, which is up dramatically from 7.9 percent in 2014—and almost three times its share in 2010 (4.4 percent). The increase in the number of DAF accounts, their total assets and grants, and, especially, the overall "market share" of DAFs as a percentage of household or individual giving demonstrate the growth of "bigger" or "big" donors. This, combined with the reality that we simultaneously saw a decline in the participation rates in giving by the small donors, reinforces the big donors' growth and the small donors' disappearance.

As the magnitude of donor-advised funds increases, concerns on the part of nonprofit fundraisers rises as well. A recent survey by The Center for Effective Philanthropy that gathered responses from 419 nonprofits with annual expenses ranging from $100,000 to $88 million found that 44 percent of nonprofits say that donor-advised funds hamper their ability to build relationships with donors.

The reason for this is simple. The sponsoring organization owns the money once a donation gets made to a donor-advised fund. That means that nonprofits have to deal directly with the sponsoring group for record-keeping, for instance, and communication. As any fundraiser knows, acknowledging a gift and its activities are opportunities to engage with the donor. However, as it concerns DAFs, nonprofits find themselves having to engage with sponsoring organizations' administrators.

I don't know about you, but having dealt with some administrators is a functional and transactional experience. It is not often that they care to engage in much more than the task to ensure they do what they need to do administratively.

Therefore, the relationship that one builds with a donor, especially on an emotional level since donors usually care about the causes they support, mostly disappears when they have to deal with the administrators of sponsoring organizations. For them, what they do is part of their job. It is an intellectual activity and not something that comes from the heart when you deal directly with donors who care about a particular cause.

Moreover, yes, it is in the interest of the sponsoring organization, such as Fidelity or Schwab, to have the funds under management within their institutions than perhaps working for the greater good. They have the opportunity to make a lot of money for their institutions, and I doubt that they are proactive with creating donors of DAF accounts to suggest that they give away the money in the funds. On the contrary, the more millions or billions of dollars they get to manage, the more profitability for their companies.

Consider this as well. Let's say you get a DAF contribution, and you want to demonstrate how the gift is making an impact. As a fundraiser, you have to send the reporting to the institutions, the sponsoring organization. If you have ever sent a donor report to a DAF, then you know it could be a faceless administrator who has little, if any, interest in your program.

Again, a nonprofit fundraiser's relationship with a DAF is inherently different from what they have when they deal directly with donors. Therefore, figuring out ways to create and maintain meaningful relationships with the person who made the DAF, which can be nurtured into the future, can get tricky.

More Money in Donor-Advised Funds Than Flowing Out

There is a perception that billions of dollars sit parked and not getting used to serving a greater good. As donor-advised funds amass more charitable dollars that grow in the funds than getting distributed into the communities, this could create a theoretical perception problem and a real-world challenge with nonprofits not having the money they need for their causes.

One donor-advised fund that I'm familiar with uses the metric of assets under management (AUM) to measure the fundraisers' success and their ability to continue to do good work. Without the assets under management, it would be difficult for these organizations to operate and meet their monthly budgets. Nevertheless, it is the impression of some nonprofit leaders and even smaller dollar level donors that wealth managers do well financially now that these funds are a huge source of revenue.

Because of the idea that DAF sponsoring organizations have inserted themselves as middle-persons and only added an obstacle between a donor and a charitable nonprofit, there is a lot more chatter in the philanthropic world about obtaining the money that's parked in donor-advised funds. As I mentioned earlier in the book, we have the resources to ensure that no one on the planet has to survive in extreme poverty.

In theory, the U.S. also has the financial resources to make a substantial dent against poverty and the other challenges that stem from it (e.g., poor education, lack of work opportunities, etc.). However, it will take the public pushing their political representatives and industries to change regulations or policies to turn on the spigot to get the funds moved from DAFs into charities working throughout our country's communities. In other words, this is not a situation of money, but will.

Some nonprofits are trying to figure out how to obtain a piece of the donor-advised fund largess. One way they are doing it is by creating their own donor-advised funds. Instead of watching the most significant donor-advised funds account for an ever-increasing amount of the charitable money given in the United States, nonprofits not traditionally in the business of donor-advised funds have decided, if you can't beat 'em, join 'em.

For instance, the University of Notre Dame and the Nature Conservancy, and many others have entered into the DAF fray. Additionally, companies are creating donor-advised funds, with the American Online Giving Foundation being one of the largest with $606 million in contributions in fiscal 2018.

Giving to Donor-Advised Funds

Donor-advised funds account for 12 percent of individual charitable giving in the United States.[25] However, it is clear that establishing more funds, giving donors more choices will continue and may even accelerate in a post-COVID world.

Regardless of the conversation of whether parked assets are getting used, it is clear that with growing assets in foundations and sponsoring organizations, there is an accumulation of funds in the DAFs. It goes without saying that as more nonprofits and even businesses create their own donor-advised funds, more assets that would in other times have gone to nonprofits doing programmatic work could instead get parked. Inevitably, some of those funds will go to charitable organizations. However, they may well go to them in the form of alternative gifts like the bequests and stock transfers after accumulating for years in DAFs.

So, what does this mean for fundraisers, and how can we adapt to this trend? It's essential to understand that DAFs and this trend by donors to park their money in sponsoring organizations adds another step in developing relationships with major gift donors and the tasks of receiving and acknowledging the gift.

Therefore, your nonprofit organization needs to understand how

---

25 "5 Things to Know About Donor-Advised Funds," Penelope Wang, Consumer Reports, December 07, 2019, https://www.consumerreports.org/charitable-donations/donor-advised-funds-things-to-know/

to cultivate relationships with DAF officers, wherever possible, and with the DAF donor creators—who no longer own the funds you want once they've opened a donor-advised fund. Relationships could be developed, but it takes more time and a lot more skill.

On a positive note, we know that the money is set aside in funds that allow donors to distribute gifts. Still, it's also important to realize that some DAFs have restrictions in place on which charities are eligible to receive donations.

For instance, one recent example is that Fidelity and Schwab banned gifts from their funds to NRA-Affiliated charities because of investigations that were underway. It is the policy that those donor-advised funds set up. Meaning, sponsoring organizations could decide at some point, depending on the mission, not to permit donations for your cause based on law, politics, or policy. Each donor-advised fund sets up its own policies.[26]

Major Donors and Giving to DAFs

I recently met a retired donor, and the money he gives away each year is through a donor-advised fund. Though he has $7 million in assets, he considers the DAF his sole source for charitable giving. In fact, on his death, the remaining money will pass to the donor-advised fund. Further, he decided to limit his giving to $60,000 a year based on what the DAF generates in revenue.

So, why is this important to understand?

As a fundraiser, I asked him if he would give $20,000 to a philanthropic cause. He responded that he would like to provide the $20,000, but because it would represent a third of his giving budget, he would not do it.

Think about that for a moment. Here we have someone with $7 million in assets, but a gift of $20,000 is a third of his allotted giving for the year. Because DAFs have administrators and donors have ideas from wealth managers about keeping the money growing, some donors restrict their giving to charities. They hope that someday, usually far-off into the future and, at some unknown point, to maximize their gifts by providing more based on the DAF's growth. In the meantime, charities that could use the funds now, and not someday in the future, have to do with less or none at all.

As we all know, we find ourselves at a time when the U.S. suffered

26 "Fidelity and Schwab Ban Gifts From Donor-Advised Funds to NRA-Affiliated Charities," Michael Theis, The Chronicle of Philanthropy, https://www.philanthropy.com/article/FidelitySchwab-Ban-Gifts/247656

from massive job losses caused by the pandemic, and because of it, competition increased for charitable dollars. It is my personal belief that a lot of the money parked in DAFs could have helped countless communities and people in need across our country recover. However, billions sit making more money in donor-advised funds, not doing anything for philanthropy, but only for the wealth managers who make fees on the money management. We now see donor-advised funds taking a substantial bite and market share from the intended ultimate beneficiaries' use. Is this a challenge for philanthropy? Undoubtedly the short answer is yes.

That said, don't get me wrong. Nothing is ever perfect in life, and everything comes with unintended consequences. As a professional fundraiser and donor, there are significant benefits to establishing a donor-advised fund. If I had a liquidity event and wanted to take advantage of placing a large sum of money, allowing substantial tax advantages, I would set up a DAF. The question is, can I then be a good steward of those resources and help maximize my charitable impact into the future? Or will I let that money sit and accumulate interest and dividends for something I may want to do in the future, or even when I pass through my estate?

Why DAFs Matter in Philanthropy

The question is, who is best served through the use of DAF charitable dollars? Is it the donor, or is it supposed to be philanthropic nonprofits offering services in their communities? Is it better to allow DAFs to accumulate more wealth for future gifts, or should funds instead be used in the shorter term (i.e., now)?

There is no doubt that donor-advised funds are an attractive vehicle for charitable giving for various constituents for donors. First, the DAF allows significant tax breaks and provides a team of philanthropic advisors to help donors think through their charitable giving. Second, the donor-advised fund accumulates a considerable amount of assets.

In theory, donors could use the funds in the future to make a substantial impact on their preferred causes. However, it is essential to note that the funds create a revenue source for the wealth managers when adequately managed. Third, the charities ultimately gain—in time—because money gets used for the greater good. But the question remains, is that greater good served when money sits in an account until it finally does get donated?

On March 9, 2020, the market experienced the largest plunge in the Dow Industrial Average history, which occurred in response to the COVID-19 virus. Two more significant drops followed that first one in the market as it crashed. That day, the 500 wealthiest people on the planet, including Mark Zuckerberg, Ray Dalio, and Lloyd Blankfein, lost $235.5 billion.[27]

As in years past, the market has corrections and downturns due to economic or global events that directly impact assets held under management. Assets aren't lost until they are sold, so the loss is only reflected on paper until the sale. Nevertheless, the amount of money lost "on paper" could have been used in powerful ways if it had been made available to charities through donations instead of managed in the market.

Sure, the market will make up the losses on paper, but the paper loss has a real value when the assets get sold. You have to wonder what could have gotten done with the $238.5 billion. What if it had gone to charity instead of making (or in this case, losing) money in the markets, including in DAF vehicles? Remember, the value of the DAFs was also affected because wealth managers in the market manage the funds.

I've heard DAF owners tell me that they never regretted giving charities money for use before any decline in the market. They feel that that it was the best use of their money. Still, it's hard not to look at money in your account or a DAF as anything other than something to accumulate and build.

In 2008, during the economic crisis, a donor told me how much money they lost in the market and said once the market recovered to a certain level, he would give $1,000,000 to the charity I was asking him to support. The market not only exceeded that number before it surpassed it, and as expected, he never made the gift. I often wonder how much money was lost that could have been used for medical research, feeding the homeless, creating scholarships, etc. There are real current needs that exist today—and not just in the distant future.

By the way, the reality of money getting parked for wealth management is not only true of donor-advised funds. This problem is also the same with endowments, which are invested assets as well.

I'm well aware that we need to plan and prepare for the future. Nevertheless, sometimes having money sitting idly and growing in an account does not serve anyone well. Again, all the money exists to solve the world's problems that get addressed by charities. However, it goes through a funnel from start to finish. Along the way, it gets deposited, parked, ex-

---

27 "Wealth Wipeout Reshapes Ranks of World's Richest People," Tom Metcalf, Venus Feng, and Devon Pendleton, Bloomberg, March 9, 2020, https://www.bloomberg.com/news/articles/2020-03-09/wealth-wipeout-reshapes-ranks-of-world-s-richest-billionaires

pended on operations leaving a continual void for those who ultimately need the resources today.

The purpose of identifying this significant piece of the charitable pie and its impact on fundraising are crucial to me. I've spent my life meeting with individual donors, talking about their financial plans, the plans for their kids' futures, and listening to their hearts on how they would like to leave the world in a better place.

However, putting money in a donor-advised fund seems somewhat cold. While I understand its practicality and benefits, I can't help but think that we have countless needs now and, wouldn't it be nice if those funds were in nonprofit bank accounts? Further, I can't help but believe that it takes away the immediacy of doing good, seeing those results, and it may even lend to the lack of general trust in nonprofits.

We spend so much time with financial advisors and lawyers that we've become accustomed to thinking through our assets' future. Is this, however, the best use of our money? Perhaps it is why some foundations work toward having an end time for the disbursement of all their assets. For example, a foundation I work with donated all its assets to several charities. They did not want to have the money sit indefinitely, accumulating wealth and not making a social impact—now.

Why DAFs Matter to Fundraisers

As fundraisers, we all have to understand how a donor-advised fund works. Realize that most major donors and an ever-increasing number of smaller donors now use donor-advised funds to think through their charitable giving and, at times, make anonymous gifts. Yes, this is another example of how a sponsoring organization could get in the way of building a relationship and nonprofits obtaining critical fundraising dollars. If a donor makes an anonymous gift, you will never have any idea from whom or why it ever came to you.

Still, thankfully, most gifts from donor-advised funds are not anonymous. However, as we have discussed here, donor-advised funds can certainly be barriers to conversations with the original donors. Rather than sitting down with an individual donor relating with a DAF, it is a whole experience.

I've heard many wealthy donors tell me that they wanted to teach their children how to become philanthropic, and to do so, they set up a donor-advised fund. They then allocated a certain sum of money within that donor-advised fund for the children to make decisions to give away.

While I understand the gesture by donors and parents, I can't help but think that while it does promote charity, it keeps children removed from the experience of philanthropy.

On the flip side, one can argue that assets under management could generate more money over the donor-advised fund's life than was initially invested. It is a gift that could become much more substantial with time, but could that money have had a more immediate and significant impact if it had gone to a nonprofit program now instead of in the future?

I've long told my clients that it is easy to count the amount of money that has been raised, but it's not easy to count the money that has been left on the table. This idea is accurate with donor-advised funds. Imagine, if you will, that no money went to donor-advised funds, and those same resources were all given to find a cure for a particular type of cancer rather than researchers looking for grants as they struggle to find the cure.

Imagine that instead of funds going to DAFs to grow over the years, donations were made for education. Perhaps children in need would not fall behind instead of wealthier peers who could afford modern technology (e.g., computers and software) for virtual schooling because of the pandemic. Maybe teachers in more impoverished districts could have helped even the playing field for students in need with professional development to educate students virtually. Perhaps parents who are laborers and maybe not used to working on computers as easily as some of us could have gotten training to help their children during virtual schooling from home?

Could that sum of money given today provide an immediate solution rather than a myriad of gifts coming out over the next ten years with multiple people working on finding an answer? Again, it's easy to quantify the dollar spent, but it is hard to quantify the impact in most instances and even hard to quantify missed impact due to lack of resources.

Planning for the Future

While we know that long-term planning has to be flexible and assume unforeseen circumstances, as philanthropy evolves, you have to ask yourself several questions to stay ahead. For instance, as donor-advised funds become the giving tool of not just billionaires and millionaires but also reaches to lower dollar donors, have you planned for this kind of contingency? Further, have you considered whether you will set up your donor-advised fund and have greater control of the assets and relationship with the donors? How will your fundraisers best manage the relationships with those donors who continually put money aside?

As fundraisers, we often look for excuses that some donors have not to give, and one legitimate excuse may be that they have decided to set up a donor-advised fund. How do you become part of the equation of the donors' intent? Moreover, how could you do it as wealth managers advise to leave the money to make an even more significant impact sometime in the future when the money has grown in the DAFs with the market returns?

While nonprofits have to tend to their day-to-day operations, it's essential for executive directors, board members, and fundraisers to think through these higher levels and strategic issues. As we move deeper into a data-driven and even more highly competitive landscape, the organizations that will fare the best are those that have their fingers on the pulse of what their constituents think and how they operate with charitable vehicles.

As it relates to donor-advised funds, as more people turn to technology and money management gets more democratized, nonprofits have to think and act based on how donors choose to support their causes. It's not going to be the same way as always. In short, the axiom is right, which is "follow the money."

FIVE

THE SCOOP ABOUT SOCIAL IMPACT INVESTING

"We take learnings from our work in philanthropy, which are donor-centric, to ask, what does investor-centric look like so that private equity can better be leveraged for social change?" — Clive Pedley, Giving Architects

When I started my career as a professional fundraiser and lawyer, things were much more straightforward than they are today. At least in fundraising, it seems that things were more or less direct. We were living in an analog world, and today that's well in the past. Today, we have young people who are much more in tune with the culture and social justice issues, primarily due to the easy sharing of ideas.

Also, we have people who have become wealthier than I think anyone could have imagined. Finally, we live in a globalized world. Although you may have countries putting up borders against immigration, the horse has left the barn. With the development of technology, people can communicate with others worldwide and consume enormous amounts of knowledge, data, and entertainment in different forms than in the past.

In essence, we are more social than ever before with people from around the world. We communicate in ways that our ancestors could never have imagined. Technology such as WhatsApp, Telegram, and even Facebook provides an opportunity every day for all of us to engage with friends, colleagues, and plenty of strangers. In sum, although we spend a lot of time behind a computer or mobile screens, many of us communicate in 21st Century ways that only the futurists imagined years ago.

Concerning philanthropy and nonprofits, the word "social" has crept into our everyday lexicon. As a result, the nonprofit sector is also called the "social good" industry. So much of the messaging and experiences we have today are about being social. It helps explain why nonprofit leaders are talking about social donors.

How Social Are You?

Social donors are what you would guess. They enjoy participating in social events and engaging with fundraisers and other donors through personal relationships. These relationships can be both in the digital or so-called real world.

A study completed by OneCause surveyed 1,056 donors who gave to charity through an event or peer-to-peer fundraiser. One of the results published showed that almost 25 percent of the adult U.S. population gave toward philanthropic causes identified as social donors. However, nonprofit fundraisers have to know a few other interesting realities about social donors, as highlighted in *The Nonprofit Times* article.[28]

- Social donors are not as committed to the nonprofits where they donate. That said, they want to have some familiarity with the organization.

- Social donors enjoy giving to event-based fundraisers. More importantly, social donors get asked to give by people they have relationships with, including friends (in social media and not) and families.

- 28 percent of social donors stated they would be willing to become sustaining donors.

- Social donors are more interested in impact than recognition, which is why fundraisers need to understand that fact so they can convert them beyond a one-time donation.

- Bequests, which is an essential traditional fundraising technique, is not something that social donors prioritize.

Those two final points are something that I want to highlight because they lead to a deeper trend in philanthropy, which is social impact investing. Others engage social donors to support philanthropic causes. They care about the impact. That's an important point to let sink in.

---

28 "Social Donors Are Less Committed To Cause," The Nonprofit Times, December 5, 2018, https://www.thenonprofittimes.com/technology/social-donors-are-less-committed-to-cause/

Traditional ways to give money (e.g., bequests) are not something they're interested in doing for philanthropy. I suspect that they care more about the here and now and the impact that nonprofits are making today. It's another reason why donors of all levels seek ways to support good causes not necessarily stuck in the past and old ways of thinking. One of those ways is through social impact investing.

Financial Rewards and Philanthropy

One of the most exciting social impact vehicles is social impact investing or impact investing. For major donors, in particular, there's interest in impact investing because they have the chance to make more money *and* a social impact.

One of the qualities of impact investing is that this kind of funding for social good does not have to go to nonprofits. In other words, a lot of social impact investing happens through for-profit social enterprises. Hang tight as we'll dig into that a little more a bit later. First, let's dig deeper into the meaning of social impact investing.

According to the Global Impact Investing Network (GIIN), which is one of the thought leaders in this space, defines social impact investing as follows:

> *Impact investments are investments made to generate positive, measurable social, and environmental impact alongside a financial return. Impact investments can be made in emerging and developed markets and target a range of returns from below market to market rate, depending on investors' strategic goals.*
>
> *The growing impact investment market provides capital to address the world's most pressing challenges in sectors such as sustainable agriculture, renewable energy, conservation, microfinance, and affordable and accessible essential services, including housing, healthcare, and education.*

As you can see in their definition, the person who makes such an investment should expect not only to make a social and environmental impact but also to see financial returns. These returns happen by investing in social impact funds.

Case Studies of Impact Investing

Let's look at a few of the case studies from GIIN to have a better understanding of social impact investing. Further, I want to highlight how nonprofits are not the only beneficiaries of impact investing in these brief case studies.

Healthy Neighborhoods

Healthy Neighborhoods is a nonprofit in the U.S. that was founded by a bank in 2004. The mission of this organization is to help rebuild and revitalize neighborhoods in Baltimore. Healthy Neighborhoods accomplishes its work by providing grants for community organizing, project development, and marketing. Also, it offers loans so that properties can get acquired and renovated.

In 2012, a second fund was created after the success of the first fund. The second fund was similar in size and scope to the first one. The first fund sourced $40 million to lend to potential homeowners at just below market rates so they can purchase, refinance and renovate homes in Baltimore. In the second fund, the Annie E. Casey Foundation (AECF) issued an unfunded guarantee by putting up $1 million in addition to a $25,000 grant to the nonprofit.

In conclusion, the impact investment was a success. There was small upfront capital used to expand the market. The financial return was a one-time fee of 50 basis points on the $1 million unfunded guarantee.

SunFunder

This business was founded in 2012 by Ryan Levinson, who started his career at the World Resources Institute in the U.S. The goal of SunFunder is to lead a "global energy transformation" by providing "universal access to energy" and lower the environmental impact from the production and distribution of energy.

The SunFunder Beyond Grid Fund was created with a geographic focus in the Pacific, India, and Sub-Saharan Africa. The focus was to target locals in places where communities existed off-the-grid and areas with a deficit of energy. The size of investors' investments, which included foundations, high-net-worth individuals, and private investors, ranged between $100,000 to $5 million. Between 4 and 7 percent was the rate of return for investors.

This fund is a sample of social impact investing for businesses. As in the first case study, you have institutional funders—specifically foundations—investing in these funds for a financial return to make an impact.

Is Philanthropy Dead?

The whole driving force of this book is about the future of fundraising, which one can argue has already arrived in many ways. So, as donors drive the focus of *how* and what to fund, it's easy for a fundraiser to wonder if it means the end of the nonprofit sector as we know it. Not quite.

Again, if you have experience in the industry, then you know it's been due for a shake-up for a long time. In many ways, it's great that it's finally happening, and donors, using technology and new financial vehicles, can help create and be a part of more strategic solutions.

We can only expect that there will be more rapid and substantive evolution in the years ahead. As I write this, you might think that what I'm describing only affects nonprofits with substantial financial resources and high dollar donors. As you'll soon learn, this is not accurate. Disruption is occurring in fundraising at the major gift, but also the general gift levels.

Omidyar Network

One of the earliest leaders of impact investing is the Omidyar Network. It was founded in 2004 by Pierre Omidyar, Founder, eBay, and his wife, Pam Omidyar. What makes the Omidyar Network interesting is that aside from being one of the earliest leaders of impact investing, the organization consists of a 501(c)(3) and Limited Liability Company (LLC). Meaning, the group makes traditional grants through the 501(c)(3) foundation, but it also makes investments in for-profit companies through the LLC.

An important side note here, following the discussion in Chapter Three about privacy, in 2018, the Governance & Citizen Engagement Initiative, which was part of the Omidyar Network, was spun off as an independent entity. It is now called Luminate and supports both nonprofits and for-profit businesses that promote policies and activities that help transform the public square. It focuses on four specific areas, which are:

1. Civic empowerment
2. Data and digital rights
3. Financial transparency
4. Independent media

While I'm not going to dig into Luminate, what I'm going to say is that the organization is yet another example of money (i.e., donors) driving the public agenda and putting their money based on their priorities to benefit society. For example, impact investing is gaining traction, and much more is happening to complement traditional philanthropy.

Concerns About Impact Investing in Philanthropy

As stated in an article by Stanford Social Innovation Review,[29] which I believe is a strong definition, "…investment has impact only if it *increases the quantity or quality of the enterprise's social outcomes beyond what would otherwise have occurred.*" There is a tension between what investors want to realize for their financial returns and what nonprofits or social good (e.g., social enterprises) need to make a positive social impact.

While impact investing increases as a vehicle of choice in the social good sector, there are several challenges:[30]

1. Some people say that impact investing does not complement philanthropy and can even do it harm. For instance, some foundations have started to invest in impact investment funds by using their endowments, but the financial return is lower than the market's investments. In other words, lower profits mean less money going out to charities as foundations must ensure that at least 5 percent of the value of their endowments get donated to nonprofits.

2. Other people claim that it cannot replace philanthropy, but if donors expect financial returns, they may seek to replace traditional giving methods. Meaning, investors will move from seeking success on social terms for their investment in an impact investment fund to seeking higher and higher financial returns in the impact funds as a measure of success. As noted in an article by *Financial Times*, "*There's a risk of 'impact-washing,' says Sonny Bardhan, who heads the internal strategy group at Omidyar Network, the organization established by eBay founder Pierre Omidyar. "If you slap 'impact' on the name of your fund, it may help raise more dollars, but it may be just a branding exercise.*"

---

29 "Unpacking the Impact in Impact Investing," Paul Brest & Kelly Born, Stanford Social Innovation Review, August 14, 2013, https://ssir.org/articles/entry/unpacking_the_impact_in_impact_investing

30 "How impact investing can complement but not displace philanthropy," Sarah Murray, Financial Times, June 21, 2019, https://www.ft.com/content/4fc97720-86d3-11e9-b861-54ee436f9768

Going back to what I mentioned earlier in this chapter, if you think that impact investing is only something to worry about for large groups or major gift donors, that's not the case. Impact investing, because of the awareness of financiers trained to understand social trends, is attractive to whole new generations of donors who want to invest in social good through technology and get a financial reward.

For example, Betterment is a financial investment platform for the masses. It uses artificial intelligence and human financiers to help people save, grow, and invest their money. They've developed what they call "socially responsible investing (SRI)." As a result, investors in the Betterment platform can limit exposure to companies deemed to have a negative social impact. For instance, this could be businesses that make money from workers with low labor standards or companies that harm the environment.

Coin is another company that seeks to make money for the public and do social good. The financial firm John Hancock, which has been around for a long time, backs Coin. Coin's exciting aspect is that while it seeks to ensure its customers invest in companies "making an impact in the areas" people care about, the idea was inspired by the United Nations Global Goals. Thus, people can invest in a broad portfolio of social areas, such as health, climate, shared prosperity, and smart and efficient cities. What's more, and to drive home the point that social impact investing is not only for wealthy individuals, you can open an account for as little as $50.

Another social impact opportunity exists for entrepreneurs and investors in a network named Social Venture Circle. SVC seeks, through its network of investors, to "work together toward a global economy that is regenerative, just, and prosperous for everyone." SVC works a little differently than Betterment and Coin through its membership program. While the investment is certainly more than the previous two platforms, for $2,000, members gain a lot of benefits.

For instance, investors can participate in peer circles, investment groups, networking opportunities, and an annual conference. Investors in SVC not only do social good through their investments in opportunities that help society, but they also have a lot of benefits to themselves as they get more informed about social impact investing.

Socially responsible investing seeks to reward companies that have ethical labor standards and operate sustainable businesses. While SRI is not "traditional" impact investing, it's still a tool that anyone interested in "social good" and "investing" can use. In other words, it's a chance for anyone to feel that they are making a social impact.

What the SRI does is it begins to blur the lines for people concerning traditional philanthropy and social impact investing. It could be argued by people who spend in SRI that they are doing social good, and thus, are being philanthropic. I'm sure marketers are already working on making sure it happens. It's not hard to get to a place where anyone—large or lower dollar donor—will think they are philanthropic, even if they do not practice what we fundraisers view as traditional philanthropy in the nonprofit sector.

The Definition of Philanthropy

I think it's essential to take a pause here and understand the definition of philanthropy. Once you remember the purest definition of that word, you can see how expert marketers can shift the public's thinking about the meaning of what it means to do good. As a result, we can find ourselves in a situation where less money is donated to nonprofits while more goes to for-profit companies and businesses, especially if they provide investors a financial return on that investment.

The idea of "philanthropy" originated in Ancient Greece. It is thought the writer of "Prometheus Bound," who was Aeschylus, coined the concept. In the Ancient Greeks' view, philanthropy is an elegant and simple idea, which is the "love of humanity." In other words, it means doing things that support the love of humanity by giving of your time and resources. Fast forward through the millennia, and you have our modern-day thinking of philanthropy exemplified through the nonprofit sector.

However, by understanding the original meaning of philanthropy, one could argue that so long as donors seek to invest in nonprofits and businesses that do not harm people or the environment, they are philanthropic.

Therefore, programs such as impact investing can and will be marketed as humanitarian by savvy marketers. Ultimately, we can face a situation where major donors and the general public substantially think beyond the traditional nonprofit sector for their philanthropic interests.

Impact Investing in Addition to Traditional Philanthropy

Eric Kessler, founder, principal, and senior managing director at Arabella Advisors said in the *Financial Times* article, "…it's not a zero-sum game." He is correct. Philanthropy and doing social good is not dependent on a finite source. As we have seen through the years in terms of traditional philanthropy, donors support charitable causes, and their generosity exceeds revenue from the previous years. Technology develops, and there are more opportunities for donors at all levels to make a difference in the world.

Sure, the idea that donors can make a social impact while also making money is now taking root. As a result, that means that traditional philanthropy, as we fundraisers know it, only expands and gets complimented in other ways. Vehicles such as impact investment funds do not represent any immediate danger to traditional philanthropic fundraising routes. However, what it will do is reorient donor giving. In other words, these tools will raise awareness of donors and expand the giving pipeline toward particular causes.

For example, with new opportunities, philanthropists can invest even more money into particular sectors, such as the environment and sustainability. The Global Impact Investing Network (GIIN) estimates that the impact investing market is as large as $502 billion. In theory, that's in addition to the $427.71 billion Americans gave to charity, according to Giving USA. That's nearly $1 trillion in money that can improve people's lives on our planet—coming through traditional and new social impact vehicles. That's an astounding number.

Let's go back to the United Nations Global Goals. The world has committed to improving on 17 goals by 2030. Those goals for every human life on this planet include no poverty, quality education, clean water, reduced inequality, and climate action. Let's take one of those goals, which is poverty. According to the Global Goals Q&A on their site, the economist Jeffrey Sachs calculated that the cost of eliminating extreme poverty is $175 billion per year. Secondly, it "represents less than one percent of the combined income of the richest countries in the world." Around the 17 goals, it is estimated that only 2 percent of the world GDP could make all of the plans a reality.

Now, let's go back to our philanthropic number of $427.71 billion and the impact investment market of $502 billion. We have the money. We need the will, and we have not to fear what is happening in our world or the philanthropic sector. Remembering the definition of philanthropy is love for humanity. So, it's good to explore innovative and disruptive ways to improve people's lives on the planet.

Further, there's nothing wrong with people who invest in a company that makes a social impact getting a financial return. There's also nothing wrong with traditional philanthropy in the sense of donating to a charity that moves you. There is space for both to co-exist and for nonprofit leaders not to be threatened by what's happening.

As fundraisers and nonprofit leaders, we have to be open and accept social impact investors' support if it makes strategic sense. Top business leaders and philanthropists understand that not all social good sectors lend themselves to social impact investing because no business model is associated with it.

For example, human rights are one area where we should not rely on market-based solutions, as we can see by the dust-up between the NBA and China concerning the Hong Kong protests and movements, such as Black Lives Matter. However, there are many opportunities for impact investment money because profitable business models exist concerning energy and sustainability.

We're moving quickly into a whole new world. Soon, cash will be non-existent, for example, as the world goes deeper into a digital reality. What's happening now with new ideas, platforms, and ways of operating—primarily because of technology's abilities and more and more people moving away from poverty—is something that we have to embrace. Sometimes, it's tough to move on, and we don't want to change things arbitrarily just to change them.

What's happening now in the social good sector is not going to stop. The chances are high that it will only accelerate as technology continues to help us deliver on solutions that have been intractable for years, generations, or even millennia.

Therefore, the fundraisers and nonprofits that are going to succeed in this fast-changing environment are those that embrace change. The successful ones will see opportunities in traditional philanthropy, but they'll also see it in new support methods, such as through vehicles like impact investing. As a result, when they do, their marketing and fundraising teams will seek ways to get into the conversations happening at these funds to present the work and their impact in their communities.

SIX

BLOCKCHAIN AND PHILANTHROPY: ARE YOU READY?

It is more difficult to give money away intelligently than to earn it in the first place." — Andrew Carnegie

As all levels of donors become much more immersed in technology and what's coming from it, they will be less inclined to donate to nonprofits that don't offer opportunities to give as they want. Again, this is another example of donors leading the way in the philanthropic sector. We're in an entirely digitized society. As a result, this creates enormous opportunities for donors to push things in the direction they want to see. Technology is not only allowing convenience, but it's also promoting transparency and on-demand, giving opportunities that are changing the nature of fundraising.

For instance, micro-giving is something that is now a regular occurrence. One of the best ways this gets executed is by groups that promote peer-to-peer giving. They ask their fundraisers to each raise, say, $1,000. The fundraisers then ask people they know to support them with $5, $10, $25, $50, or $100 to achieve the $1,000 goal. The fundraisers also tell people what the money will do (i.e., the impact) for a cause.

Donors then participate in the micro-giving campaign. Once the $1,000 gets achieved, people experience what psychologists call the "completion effect."[31] People and donors love the idea of seeing the impact of something they are supporting—quickly. Think of it like a sugar high. Peer-to-peer giving allows donors to support their favorite causes and then feel a sense of accomplishment upon achieving their fundraising goal. They think they've done something good to make an impact.

Today's donor thinks differently, and technology allows for innova-

---

31 "Why Smaller Donations Are One of 2019's Biggest Online Fundraising Trends," Daryl Hatton, GuideStar Blog, February 4, 2019, https://trust.guidestar.org/why-smaller-donations-are-one-of-2019s-biggest-online-fundraising-trends

tive and donor-centric methods of giving, which will ultimately give donors more power. In other words, the savvy tech companies, along with marketers, understand that human behavior is essential for success. So, they create opportunities for "reward" for people that keep them coming back. They also push positive social values, such as transparency and impact, which most people believe are good attributes for people and organizations.

As all of this evolves—quickly—we have good things and bad things that happen. For example, we know now that social media can be addictive. Also, we understand that we can create much more significant results for the better than at any other time in human history concerning nonprofit missions and social causes. As people understand the abilities and positive outcomes within their reach, what drives people to give for a social cause also changes. There's a race taking place to innovate and capture success—including for social good purposes—based on human behaviors enabled with technology.

Stock Ownership and Philanthropy

American ownership in stock is increasing because of the ease of technology. In the digital world, anyone with an extra $50 to spare can open an account. Thus, more than 50 percent of Americans own stock,[32] And they are learning and enjoying the benefits of investing in the market.

Reporters say that there are a variety of reasons for this increase in stock ownership. For instance, index and mutual funds have become safer, easier, and more popular. Also, there's the investment by people in retirement funds. However, I think there's an additional reason. Investing is democratized. As noted in the previous chapter, you have platforms such as Betterment and Coin for little money investments. Those platforms also use technology and data, which takes a lot of the mystery out of investing for Americans. With artificial intelligence making investment decisions, it's easy to set it and forget it.

As investing becomes even more democratized, anyone can participate in the proper American sport of making money. Enter blockchain. Fundraisers, who deal with donors all day long, have heard of blockchain. Hopefully, you have as well, because if you are genuinely thinking about the "future of fundraising," which in reality is now, you understand that the old ways of doing things are dying.

---

32 "Americans own more stock than ever—how will it change the economy?" Allison Shrager, Quarz, September 5, 2019, https://qz.com/1700958/more-americans-own-stock-than-ever/

Also, donors continue to lead the way they use new technologies and platforms developed for the social good space. The charities that will thrive are those that understand the ever-changing landscape. The non-profits that do not adapt or continue to keep their heads in the sand, as if it's still the year 2000, will inevitably tread water and potentially close.

Let's take a look at some of the realities we live with now. People use their phones every day to pay for items. Meaning, many no longer carry wallets with them. For years, seniors received Social Security checks through bank transfers. I don't know when the last time I wrote a check was; I'm sure the same holds for you. Do people write checks anymore?

Thus, as so much about our existence becomes digitized—fully—fundraisers and nonprofit leaders who want to thrive must forget about the "future" and remember that "the future" is now. Concerning blockchain, are you ready to process donations using this technology? If not, don't worry. This chapter will help you understand blockchain and how it is disrupting philanthropy. The nonprofits that survive are those that adapt and integrate new ideas and technologies into their organizations.

What in the World is Blockchain?

Before we can understand how blockchain can disrupt philanthropic giving, we have to understand its meaning. Also, it's essential to remember that technology is a great disrupter. Because of it, it's allowing anyone—not just the wealthy—to exist in ways that have never lived in human history. Communication, for instance, is one of the best examples of it. Today, anyone can send a tweet, publish a post, or send money worldwide with the press of a button on phones.

I found one of the best explanations of blockchain in an old article.[33] Because I'm a fundraiser and not a technology expert, I'll share the most salient points below. I have bolded for emphasis.

> By allowing digital information to be distributed **but not copied**, blockchain technology created the backbone of a new type of internet. Initially devised for the **digital currency, Bitcoin (Buy Bitcoin)**, the tech community has found other potential uses for the technology....
> In the simplest of terms, **a blockchain is a time-**

33 "What is Blockchain Technology? A Step-by-Step Guide For Beginners," Ameer Rosic, Blockgeeks, https://blockgeeks.com/guides/what-is-blockchain-technology/

stamped series of immutable records of data that is managed by a cluster of computers not owned by any single entity. Each of these blocks of data (i.e., block) is secured and bound to each other using cryptographic principles (i.e., chain)...

The blockchain network has no central authority — it is the very definition of a democratized system. Since it is a shared and immutable ledger, the information in it is open for anyone and everyone to see. Hence, anything that is built on the blockchain is by its very nature transparent, and everyone involved is accountable for their actions...

One party to a transaction initiates the process by creating a block. This block is verified by thousands, perhaps millions of computers distributed around the net. The verified block is added to a chain stored across the net, creating a unique record and a unique record with a unique history...

But the key here is this: it's free. Not only can the blockchain transfer and store money, **but it can also replace all processes and business models that rely on charging a small fee for a transaction.** *Or any other transaction between two parties.*

Let's start to bring this down to your fundraising experience. In the simplest form, let's say that a donor contributes, and you are one of the nonprofit leaders that accept blockchain. When your donor makes that gift, the information stored in the block is the date, time, and amount of the contribution. The donor's information gets verified against public records. However, the donor's name is recorded as a "digital signature," which is not the actual name. The transaction itself receives a code, which is called a "hash." Think of the hash as the receipt number. Once the "block" gets added to the "blockchain," it's public information, and you can see Bitcoins blockchain publicly.[34]

Hold On! Is Bitcoin Private?

The obvious question based on the previous section is whether or not the blockchain is private when all blockchains are publicly viewable. The short

---

34 BTC Blocks, https://www.blockchain.com/btc/blocks

answer is that all blockchains are visible on the internet, but there is privacy. Remember, the name of the person initiating the transaction gets converted into a "digital signature." In other words, their name can be hidden, yes, even from your nonprofit.

What's more, people can opt to connect their computers to blockchain networks and get updates as a democratizing force. The fact that there are, in theory, millions of people with copies of any particular blockchain makes it much harder for hackers to corrupt. In other words, they would have to corrupt or hack every one of the millions of copies of the blockchain, which is a good thing.

Suppose you would like to know more about blockchain, including privacy and security. In that case, you can take a look at *Investopedia's* "Blockchain Explained,"[35] or other resources on the internet. Let's take a look at the idea and reality of blockchain in the philanthropic sector.

It's All About Transparency

Blockchain serves as yet another reminder that we live in a world filled with transparency for most. Sure, we also know that transparency for the world's largest tech companies, such as Google or Facebook, does not necessarily occur as they build out their technology. Nevertheless, the idea of transparency is promulgated as a good thing. When we take the concept of transparency into the philanthropic world, we hear the following:

- Transparency
- Impact
- Results

In other words, donors have become less inclined to give to nonprofit groups that are not transparent. Consequently, because nonprofits operate as tax-exempt groups, in the public trust, that's as it should be. Who wants to support a nonprofit group and make any contribution only to see it go into a black hole at an organization that is opaque?

Blockchain is yet another idea (e.g., social media, impact investments) that further pushes the notion of transparency. Again, every transaction and block created is "transparent" and publicly visible. Even if the person who initiates the transaction is seen only through the digital signature, the idea remains. Just as our names, Social Security numbers, credit card numbers, etc., have become our identifiers, so too the digital signa-

---

35 "Blockchain Explained," Investopedia, https://www.investopedia.com/terms/b/blockchain.asp

tures identify us.

Therefore, it stands to reason that as people become more transparent—and demand it from corporations, and yes, nonprofits—the organizations that survive and thrive are those that adhere to the collective idea about transparency. Again, for nonprofits with their unique tax-exempt and social good status in society, they have an even greater obligation for transparency. Donors will make sure that they do, and in fact, it's something that they've been demanding for a long time. In the many discussions I've had with donors, there is a recurrent theme about nonprofits being held accountable for demonstrating transparency and impact.

In a world where donors demand that nonprofits be transparent, impact-driven, and results-oriented, blockchain offers them an opportunity to push nonprofits harder. For instance, let's take a look at nonprofits that operate globally. Unless you leave the U.S., the chances are that you may not be aware of how much money gets lost in transaction fees and costs for converting different currencies. Let's say that a donor in the U.S. would like to make a $100 donation to a global children's charity operating out of Europe. Or, perhaps a U.S. nonprofit has operations in developing countries as the focus of its mission. Every time money crosses borders, several "middlemen" take their cut from that money. So, that $100 or donation becomes 90,80 Euros at the current rate as of this writing. That's a significant loss of money.

As I explained earlier, blockchain takes out all middle folks, such as the banks or currency exchange platforms. The costs for that $100 donation decrease significantly. Remember, blockchain is free. There are zero costs for transactions, although there could be costs for infrastructure. There's something even more important to remember about blockchain; donors can see how the money gets used and trace their money all along the way.

In the next section, we'll look at a few of the real-world nonprofit case studies of blockchain at work in the philanthropic sector.

Real-world Cases of Blockchain in the Philanthropic Sector

As illustrated by Stanford Graduate School of Business, Center for Social Innovation, in collaboration with RippleWorks,[36] They reported on the

---

36 Blockchain for Social Impact: Moving Beyond the Hype," Stanford Graduate School of Business, Center for Social Innovation, in partnership with RippleWorks, https://www.gsb.stanford.edu/sites/gsb/files/publication-pdf/study-blockchain-impact-moving-beyond-hype.pdf

fund management platform called Disberse. Blockchain was used through the Disberse platform for the charitable group Positive Women. The nonprofit lowered its transfer fees by two-and-a-half percent in support of educational projects in Swaziland.

Also, the U.N. World Food Program has used blockchain to pay vendors. That use reduced their bank transfer fees by an astounding 98 percent in its pilot. Considering it spends as much as $6 billion every year, the savings are enormous, in the range of tens of millions of dollars.

However, blockchain is doing more than saving money for nonprofits operating globally. It's also providing nonprofit groups and donors with new ways to support their favorite causes through crowdfunding platforms and "tokenized giving." Most people know about crowdfunding with platforms such as JustGiving, GoFundMe, and others. Without getting too deep in the weeds here for tokenized giving, assets (e.g., money, stock, real estate, etc.) get issued a blockchain security token. That token represents the tradeable asset.[37] So, tokenized giving is when nonprofits receive that token, which for our example, can represent money, stock, or another tradeable asset.

Since 2015, when Fidelity Charitable started accepting cryptocurrency for donations, it has received more than $106 million. In 2018 alone, they received $30 million. As they wrote in their report, *"Fidelity Charitable's ability to accept cryptocurrency donations, including bitcoin, allowed these donors to eliminate any capital gains taxes and give the full fair market value to charity."*

Nevertheless, you might be thinking to yourself that the people who donate through Fidelity Charitable tend to be wealthier donors. Yes, that is true. However, remember that technology is democratizing many aspects of our world, including giving. Platforms such as BitGive and PinkCoin allow anyone to make any donation. Let's take a quick look at these two platforms as examples of what's happening.

BitGive

This platform seeks to "revolutionize global philanthropy through technology," which they accomplish by leveraging Bitcoin and blockchain. The company was founded in 2013 and was incorporated as a 501(c)(3)—

---

37 "The tokenization of assets is disrupting the financial industry. Are you ready?" Patrick Laurent, Thibault Chollet, Michael Burke, Tobias Seers, Deloitte.com, https://www2.deloitte.com/content/dam/Deloitte/lu/Documents/financial-services/lu-tokenization-of-assets-disrupting-financial-industry.pdf

meaning that it is a nonprofit—and I would suggest one of what will be a new breed of organizations. The charity seeks to improve the lives of people through its focus on public health and the environment. It sees itself as a group that is "bridging the gap between an innovative technology and its practical applications for nonprofits and humanitarian work in the developing world."

One of the other aspects of the nonprofit, which I believe is essential to include, is that it has partnered with global nonprofits such as Save the Children, The Water Project, and Medic Mobile. Further, in 2015, BitGive created Bitcoin Charity 2.0 Initiative. The project aims to leverage blockchain technology as a donation platform for nonprofits around the world. Also, if you take a look at its site and the Initiative, you'll see that they promote transparency "by sharing financial information and direct project results in real-time." As noted earlier in this chapter, transparency is in sharp relief.

PinkCoin

Pinkcoin used blockchain to support nonprofit and social good organizations, encouraging their communities' support and participation. As of the writing of this book, nearly $25.5 million got processed through its platform. Its platform, Donate4Life, is a fundraising pool, and monies get disbursed by donors through the platform to their partners.

Through the technology created by PinkCoin, donors can support humanitarian, environmental, educational, disaster relief, and charitable causes through its pools. You can take a look at its dynamic pools for giving by visiting https://donate.with.pink/. I suggest you take a look to familiarize yourself with blockchain for philanthropy.

Walls Coming Down

The idea of Bitcoin and blockchain for philanthropy is significant. And I believe it's most notable because these technologies and approaches allow people to make a social impact, but not necessarily with a nonprofit. While it's true that nonprofits such as Save the Children and the Red Cross have accepted blockchain for their missions, it's also true that what defines "social good" projects are no longer limited to the work of nonprofits.

The fundraising evolution is not limited to raising money for a good cause through nonprofits or social enterprises (including for-profit groups). One of the exciting developments or ideas concerning blockchain is related to foundations, more precisely "crypto-foundations."[38] The Pine-apple Fund was an experiment in cryptocurrency philanthropy. A wealthy donor decided to donate to causes they cared about around the world. The giving occurred during the peak of the cryptocurrency bubble in 2017. The result was that the anonymous donor supported 60 charities with 5,104 Bitcoins, which was $55 million. If you do a simple Google search, you will see much discussion about "decentralized" giving; that is, giving in ways that do not require any traditional foundations or nonprofits.

Another impressive group is the Blockchain Charity Foundation. The mission of this foundation is to "improve the lives of the 'bottom billion' through blockchain technology." It is the belief of those who founded the foundation that it takes the market and philanthropy to find sustainable solutions for people in need. They seek to get to the root cause so that the people they help can entirely escape poverty.

As you know, systemic poverty has so many strains to it—lack of jobs, education, resources at home, medical, etc. Further, the foundation seeks to "bring the benefits of this revolution to the people who had no access to technology innovation before." In other words, they give to charity and fully involve those they help with the ability to use modern-day necessities, such as technology.

Of note for this foundation, the cryptocurrency donated goes directly to the end-user, and it does not pass through nonprofit groups. As a result, people who need support get technology and cryptocurrency wallets through smartphones to use what gets given. Further, donors and the public can get a transparent look at how the currency is spent. The middle person nonprofit or NGO is out of the process. As a result, decentralized giving allows people to give to others directly in transparent and potentially more rewarding ways. Other examples of decentralizing giving include the GiveDirectly, GiveCrypto, and BitHope.

While at present, the number of donors who are giving in these ways to charity remains much smaller compared to traditional methods of giving, but it won't last for long. Millennials and Generation Z, as you probably know, are the largest generations living. Millennials were introduced early to the digital world, and Gen Z is the first natively digital generation from the moment of their birth.

---

38 **"Crypto-philanthropy: How Bitcoin and Blockchain Are Disrupting the World of Giving," Paul Lamb, Medium, February 12, 2018,** https://medium.com/@pauljlamb/crypto-philanthropy-how-bitcoin-and-blockchain-are-disrupting-the-philanthropic-sector-80716dc7cb68

These two generations are massive in size and operate in a digital world first means that there are immense opportunities for decentralized giving through blockchain and other technologies. Both of these generations have been early adopters because they trust and operate entirely in the digital world. Therefore, nonprofit leaders need to understand that Millennial and Gen Z donors will drive change—it's inevitable.

Philanthropy will not only evolve; it is in the process of going through what will become a revolution. The ways to support good causes now mean opportunities, through the cloud, to help people and their causes directly—not with nonprofit staff in offices. Think about that. It's a profound idea.

2020 saw the world deal with a global pandemic, but one of the fascinating aspects was how it changed how businesses, including nonprofits, operated. All of a sudden, organizations said they were going remote in whole or in part. Not having to spend funds anymore on office costs and space is a great money saver. In the process, groups shifted to working in virtual areas, and even fundraisers changed as nonprofits sought ideas to raise money that did not involve in-person events.

As we all know, history shifts and changes. It would be arrogant of us in the nonprofit sector to think that new generations will maintain things as we created or left them. Why should they do that? Why can't inventors generate platforms for people to give directly to one another in a modern world heavily reliant and lived in cyberspace? Just because we formalized nonprofits in the 19th and 20th Centuries, why should future generations continue to rely on those vehicles to provide to others in need?

While these questions may seem rhetorical, in many ways, they are not because the evolution (and revolution) has already started bringing to us the capabilities of technology and innovative thinking for the modern era. Decentralized giving, because of technology such as blockchain, means that donors have the opportunity to give to people directly. There is zero need to give to a charity—if a donor doesn't want to donate in that fashion. The donor can simply send money, including blockchain, to someone on the other side of the planet directly without any need for a nonprofit team to be in the middle of the transaction.

Further, when you have 1 in 3 Americans distrustful of charities[39]—

---

39 "1 in 3 Americans Lacks Faith in Charities, Chronicle Poll Finds," Suzanne Perry, The Chronicle of Philanthropy, October 5, 2015, https://www.philanthropy.com/article/1-in-3-Americans-Lacks-Faith/233613

as they are of many institutions, such as government and the press—what prevents younger generations from dispensing with nonprofits all together in the future? As was noted in the published report by Stanford Graduate School of Business, Center for Social Innovation and RippleWorks,

> *One of the issues hindering giving and aid is a lack of transparency, and, therefore, often a lack of trust that funds will be used effectively. Currently, billions get donated to a recipient organization, agency, or government. Once the money leaves the donor's account, there is limited tracking or transparency available to determine exactly how the funds were used and who ultimately benefited. Donors are also becoming more results- and impact-focused and trust in the recipient organization is crucial to their giving decision-making.*
>
> *According to a survey by Fidelity Charitable, 41% of donors say they have changed their giving due to increased knowledge about nonprofit effectiveness.*

Some donors, who may not trust nonprofits, seek to find other ways to give, and because of innovation and technology, they have more choices for doing so. For example, I have a friend who lives in Europe, and she was a fundraiser in the United States for many years. However, as many good things as she saw during her years as a fundraiser, she also saw things—such as serious financial mismanagement at nonprofits—that caused great concern. She continues to be philanthropic.

However, she and her husband have moved toward giving directly to people in need when possible, and they have also started to explore other ways to support people directly. If they do give to charity, they only do so to transparent and clear organizations concerning their financials and performance metrics. Typically, this means giving to larger groups as the vast majority of small nonprofits are only treading water. When they see an opportunity to give directly to someone, they do, so they can more directly enjoy the joys of giving and make a difference. As they learn about other ways to support a good cause, they are looking to shift their giving in the coming years from traditional methods to modern techniques with much more transparency and opportunity for impact.

While my friend and her husband are only two people, they are not alone. In the conversations I've had with donors along the way, they're open to exploring modern ideas and technologies to meet their need for seeing a social impact. They are testing new approaches and are not afraid to try different things. One major donor I spoke to suggested that as a donor, nonprofit leaders will accept his demands for transparency and demonstrated impact, or he will go through them or around them.

Why Blockchain Matters—It's a Shift in the Donor Mentality

Blockchain offers donors an incredible opportunity. Donors are looking more critically at how they can support causes in more transparent ways. They seek more efficiencies in their giving, and they are looking to lead social good change.

In a later chapter, you will learn about the modern-day donor mindset, which includes more significant impact, new ideas, and transparency. That transparency, by the way, consists of both how monies get spent and also the impact made. In other words, for the gifts they make in the spirit of changing lives, they want to see the changes happen.

Blockchain is one of the tools that can bring a lot of change to donors, especially those who are comfortable operating digitally. Binance Academy explained the opportunities for donors and charities that choose to be transparent. Those advantages include the following:[40]

- *Total transparency: each cryptocurrency transaction is unique, which means it is also easily tracked through the blockchain. The higher level of transparency and public accountability can ease donors' minds and encourage them to give while reinforcing the charity's reputation for integrity.*

- *Global and decentralized: most blockchain networks present high levels of decentralization, meaning that they do not need to rely on a centralized government or other institutions. Thus, funds can move directly from donors to charities, and the decentralized nature of blockchain makes it uniquely suitable for international transactions.*

- *Digital agreements: blockchain makes it easier to share and store digital data and may also be used to ensure that relevant documents or contracts cannot be modified without all involved members' approval.*

---

40 "Blockchain Uses: Charity," Binance Academy, December 23, 2019, https://www.binance.vision/blockchain/blockchain-use-cases-charity

- *Reduced expenses: blockchain technology has the potential to simplify the way charities are managed, automating parts of the process and reducing the overall costs by requiring fewer intermediaries.*

- *Reduced taxes: considering a US-based donor as an example, if a contribution gets made with Bitcoin, the charity will get the full donated value (no capital gain taxes). Moreover, the donor would be able to claim a higher tax deduction towards governmental agencies.*

Sure, just as there are opportunities, there are also risks, as noted in the article. For example, cryptocurrencies get traded in volatile markets. If private keys get lost, they are lost, and there's no way to recover those funds. Finally, the fact that most people don't understand cryptocurrencies is a challenge. However, with time, things get perfected. There's no reason to think that these risks will not minimize and get addressed in the coming years. That becomes especially true when you have people who think the risk is worth the reward, convenience, and transparency they will experience using new ways of giving.

In sum, while the number of people exploring modern ways of giving, such as blockchain, is small compared to traditional philanthropic giving, the fact of the matter is that disruption and innovation are taking root. When you have an institution such as Fidelity Charitable accept cryptocurrencies, you know there's no going back to cash and checks. That said, one of the driving forces—and attractiveness—of blockchain is the transparency it offers. Ultimately, I expect that donors will continue to push nonprofits and groups where they charitably give to be more transparent about finances and impact metrics.

Finally, what is evolving are opportunities for donors to deal directly with recipients. As time passes, you have to wonder if there will be a wholesale shift away from nonprofits and charities toward decentralized giving in future generations. From the donors' perspective, it makes a lot of sense because they get much more transparency and the chance to see—closely and more intimately—what happens as they try to improve others' lives. Only time will tell how things develop, but as Bob Dylan wrote, "… *the times they are a changin'.*"

SEVEN

DIRTY LITTLE SECRETS ABOUT FUNDRAISER COMPENSATION

"Giving is not just about making a donation. It is about making a difference." — Kathy Calvin

I've been a fundraiser for many years. So, that has given me the chance to speak to other fundraisers through the years. There's one problem that many fundraisers—and I mean a lot—and other nonprofit professionals talk about as a challenge. If you guessed salary and compensation, well, then you guessed correctly. The topic of low wages in the industry has been around for decades. While change is happening, as we'll see in this chapter, overall, the industry has to do better by its people.

Here's the reality: nonprofits are supposed to serve the betterment of people. However, it's no secret that many fundraisers and nonprofit teams do not receive competitive salaries, and the current economic climate might make matters worse. Additionally, nonprofit leaders expect workers who have a passion for the mission to work until the "job" gets finished.

So, what ends up happening is that in smaller nonprofits in particular, under the regulatory radar, you have countless fundraisers working long nights and weekends—essentially for free—to ensure that the gala, fundraising event, or donor meetings get done. In other words, they work without compensation to ensure that the nonprofit raises as much money as possible. But, because the places where they work happen to be small or have low revenues, they don't have to adhere to state or federal laws on wages, and people go uncompensated.

Some of the stories I've heard not only include staff working for free but also deferring necessary health care. As we all know too well, healthcare requires an overhaul, but that's another story. Nevertheless, people in the social good sector have been known to defer medical care because they earn so little that it's the rent and food or high medical premiums from medical procedures. There have been others who have worried about childcare due to late nights or weekend work because other family members are also working or they're single heads of households.

If you've worked in the nonprofit sector for some time, then you probably heard about the compensation issue from colleagues or read about it in countless articles. In this chapter, I want to put fundraisers and nonprofit staff compensation on the table. Often, it's a mystery to donors who don't realize what's happening. Then, I want to talk about solutions that can help make things better.

Reasons for Low Compensation

It's a reality that thousands of people enter the nonprofit field every year, wanting to make a positive impact. However, in time, they get disillusioned because it's tough to live with a salary below the market rate. For the most part, I'll focus on fundraisers because there's a revolving door for those positions. Nevertheless, generally, when nonprofits pay fundraisers (who raise the money to operate), they're paying other staff members poorly as well.

According to a published infographic[41] by Bloomerang and Mazarine Treyz of Wild Woman Fundraising, the nonprofit sector's turnover rate is 19 percent. Also, they reported that fundraisers left their positions after only approximately 16 to 18 months on the job. As you would think, this has real costs to the nonprofits they exit. One of those costs is financial. Also reported were the associated direct and indirect costs to nonprofits—$127,650, based on the research of Penelope Burk, every time a fundraiser leaves the organization. Those are significant expenses.

A few years earlier, DB&A, an executive search firm, published a study[42] that said, 91 percent of large nonprofit associations experienced fundraising turnover. We have a problem in the nonprofit sector. So, why has all of this been happening? As DB&A noted, half of the fundraisers surveyed said they were looking to leave the organization within two years. 53 percent of nonprofits had trouble finding qualified fundraisers for their group. As a fundraiser, I can tell you that you're losing opportuni-

---

41 "[INFOGRAPHIC] State of the Nonprofit Workplace 2019," Kristen Hay, Bloomerang, February 5, 2019, https://bloomerang.co/blog/infographic-state-of-the-nonprofit-workplace-2019/

42 "Five Ways to Fix the Turnover Problem in Your Fundraising Department," Derric Bakker, DB&A Executive Search & Recruitment, September 4, 2017, https://nonprofit-executive-search.com/insights/fix-fundraising-staff-turnover

ties and money for your cause every day you don't have someone leading fundraising.

There are several reasons for the turnover, in my opinion, which I will outline for you here. By doing so, I hope to inform you, the reader, about the persistent challenge of fair and equitable pay of nonprofit professionals. I also want to lend my voice to other industry leaders who say that enough is enough. It's not credible to claim that our missions are about social good and bettering society, but then we underpay our employees as an industry. Those two positions are not mutually exclusive and must be reconciled, particularly in an era that is about transparency and fairness.

Internal Revenue Service

One of the top reasons many nonprofit professionals don't get paid well is the IRS. Now, I'm not at all saying that the IRS has to do anything more than it's doing. However, I am saying that many nonprofit leaders use the IRS rule about "reasonable compensation" as an excuse. I've heard from fundraisers that a board member typically cites the IRS term "reasonable compensation." It suggests that fundraisers could not earn what board members considered an "unreasonable" salary—even though nonprofit compensation studies for the industry showed that these fundraisers could receive more.

The IRS guidelines state, *"Reasonable compensation is the value that would ordinarily be paid for like services by like enterprises under like circumstances. Reasonableness is determined based on all the facts and circumstances."*[43] In other words, reasonableness gets measured in varying ways, despite the availability of compensation reports for the industry. Therefore, one of the best things any nonprofit professional can do during salary discussions is to obtain the latest compensation reports published by organizations such as Guidestar, The Nonprofit Times, National Council of Nonprofits, or Bridgespan. However, others exist, which are also good and may also be local to your city or region of the country. The bottom line, however, is that all nonprofit professionals should always know their worth.

Further, nonprofit leaders have to begin their work by looking internally and supporting their teams with living and competitive wages.

---

43 "Exempt Organization Annual Reporting Requirements: Meaning of "Reasonable" Compensation," Internal Revenue Service (IRS), https://www.irs.gov/charities-non-profits/exempt-organization-annual-reporting-requirements-meaning-of-reasonable-compensation

Association of Fundraising Professionals (AFP)

One of the other challenges in the industry is the association that is supposed to look out for their professional members' welfare and professional development. The Association of Fundraising Professionals (AFP), Code of Ethics,[44] which was adopted in 1964, by the way, has various elements that work against fundraisers.

First, it says that both individuals and organizations should aspire to "Put philanthropic mission above personal gain." While the idea is commendable, in practice, it offers another opportunity for nonprofit leaders and board members to suggest that "personal gain" (i.e., a competitive salary) is not a good thing. In my opinion, the idea needs updated language after decades of seeing where it has led the industry.

Below is the section for the Members of the AFP related to compensation. I'm noting it below in full, so there is nothing taken out of context.

Members shall:

21. not accept compensation or enter into a contract based on a percentage of contributions; nor shall members accept finder's fees or contingent fees.

22. be permitted to accept performance-based compensation, such as bonuses, only if such bonuses are in accord with prevailing practices within the members' own organizations and are not based on a percentage of contributions.

23. neither offer nor accept payments or special considerations for the purpose of influencing the selection of products or services.24. not pay finder's fees, commissions, or percentage compensation based on contributions.

25. meet the legal requirements for the disbursement of funds if they receive funds on behalf of a donor or client.

Let's dissect the commission or performance-based compensation argument. Should nonprofit fundraisers earn a commission based on a percentage of what they raise? According to industry norms, the answer is no. However, that's short-sighted, and it contributes to the fact that we have plenty of fundraisers who claim to be major gift officers but who, candidly,

---

44 "Association of Fundraising Professionals, Code of Ethical Principles," Adopted 1964, https://afpglobal.org/ethicsmain/code-ethical-standards

don't genuinely know and practice the skills for raising that kind of money. They don't understand the delicate balance of cultivating a relationship, and when the moment arrives to make the "right" (i.e., amount) ask, they don't. However, in my view, this lack of training and expertise is not reflective of those fundraisers. It is reflective of the nonprofit that doesn't make the necessary investment in its people to pay well, and yes, train fundraisers properly.

Board members and people in the business will tell you that we don't want "hired guns" because nonprofit donors won't give to them. Well, I've made more than 4,000 solicitations in my career, engaged with others to raise over $1 billion, and I can tell you that most of the asks I've made have been as a "hired gun." Getting back to the idea of no "personal gain," let's face it, when people get paid, there is a personal interest and "gain." I don't mean to parse words here, but in my estimation, it wouldn't hurt to give a salary base, plus commission, to nonprofit fundraisers. Several nonprofits currently implement this compensation structure. As a nonprofit fundraiser, I believe that professionals have to get paid and incentivized to perform; they will rise to the challenge and become the best in their profession.

Fundraisers like to say that fundraising is a "team effort." While that's true to a certain extent, let's say, for instance, when board members or major donors provide introductions, an ask is made by one person or by two people. That should be rewarded because asking for money is a skill that many people—even fundraisers—don't necessarily possess. Moreover, suppose you don't have a fundraiser who asks major donors for money on the team. In that case, the amount of time and strategy development that goes into raising money from corporations, small-dollar donors, or events should nevertheless get rewarded. Depending on each professional's involvement or position within an organization, nonprofits can create incentivized pay scales for their employees.

Another argument against getting commissions is that fundraisers would focus on the prospects who have the most to give, leaving the nonprofit vulnerable. Again, this is an argument that is a little too seemingly clever. The reality is that you *want* your fundraisers to focus on donors *and* revenue streams that garner the most funds. Do you want your fundraisers to waste time (and money) on people and streams of income that won't produce the best results? As an industry, we should ensure that nonprofits have diversified revenue streams to hedge against downturns. That makes sense and can get incorporated into an annual fundraising plan.

However, the reality is that if nonprofit leaders and board members make it clear in their goals and objectives that fundraisers focus on diversified risk, it will get done. So, paying fundraisers a base plus a commission will only motivate the best fundraisers to perform. No one is suggesting that nonprofit fundraisers earn millions. Still, compensation plans can get crafted to provide fundraisers with a modicum of security with a base salary and motivation for increased earnings with a commission or incentivized pay.

Lack of Understanding by Donors, Nonprofit Boards—and the Public

Have you noticed that eventually, people will believe something when you say it often enough, even a lie? That's why we live in an era of "fake news." Everything is "fake"—only it's not. Facts still do matter, as does nuance, subtly, and context. As a lawyer, if a client asked me to represent them, perhaps to determine where they should contribute, I would review and analyze a few things, including the facts about the mission where they want to donate, financials, and the impact.

I would also get familiar with the best nonprofits doing that work by analyzing the management team's backgrounds and board. I would research and understand the impact (qualitative and quantitative) that they're making. Finally, I would do some more due diligence by asking around and speaking to others. In other words, facts matter, and so does reality.

The reality is that it's too convenient for the nonprofit sector to say that they have to keep pay low to ensure that funds go to the mission. It's just not an accurate statement to make. What donors want is success. They want to ensure the mission of a nonprofit, and that improves as many lives as possible. That's only accomplished by hiring, and retaining, talented professionals. Therefore, educating donors about the challenges nonprofit staff have in living their lives would go a long way toward turning people's hearts and minds. The public is not getting educated, as it should, about the sacrifices that people make to work in the nonprofit industry.

I firmly believe that if donors and the public understood what happens with many workers in the sector and how paying workers little goes against what should be happening (i.e., innovation, impact, success), there would be a donor-led movement to change things. Unfortunately, I don't think organizations believe it's in their interest to be frank and real with donors, supporters, and the public. In some way, many nonprofit leaders think showing how little they spend on operational costs, including salaries, is the right approach to getting fundraising dollars. However, all this is doing is creating a space for social enterprises and for-profit businesses to talk about "investment" and to far outpace and innovate for social change.

Fast Company published a short, excellent piece[45] about nonprofit pay. As the author rightly stated, people think that working at a nonprofit should be the "reward." As if doing social good means that you shouldn't get paid for your work. In that case, anyone who did something that benefits people (e.g., doctors) should not benefit. Their reward should be the fact that they're helping people. As the article highlighted, low nonprofit pay hurts morale. Nonprofit professionals, especially women, earn significantly less than what similar roles would make in other industries. Because of the compensation challenge, there's a "disconnect" between how many nonprofits operate and the social good missions. That stands to reason because nonprofit teams also have bills to pay.

I'll add that institutional donors, such as foundations, also have rules against paying via a commission. As a result, that means that nonprofits that want to get donations from these organizations can't pay fundraisers with a commission. I'm not suggesting we pay fundraisers straight commission only. However, I am saying that we can have a salary plus a commission or bonus incentive. When positioned as such, you will find that many foundations support the idea.

All of this can be rolled up neatly into the "overhead myth" obsession dogging the sector for decades. Simply, boards, nonprofit founders, donors, and the public have pushed nonprofits to spend as little as possible. Therefore, think of the first place where nonprofit leaders decided not to spend money. If you guessed nonprofit salaries, well again, you guessed correctly. Nonprofit teams have generally gotten the short end of the stick, and everyone suffers because of this nonsense idea. The relentless overhead myth idea that nonprofits (unlike for-profit businesses) can't spend on their operating costs has accomplished the following:

- It's limited innovation and scalability.
- The idea has prevented talented people from entering or remaining in the field and instead work in the for-profit sector.
- The overhead myth has kept passionate and talented nonprofit

---

45 "At nonprofits, the 'reward' for work still isn't money," Ben Paynter, Fast Company, June 12, 2019, https://www.fastcompany.com/90360852/at-nonprofits-the-reward-for-work-still-isnt-money

professionals as second-class citizens continually looking for an opportunity to work for social good but get paid a sustainable living wage (hence the revolving door).

- The idea of having everything—including salaries—on a shoe-string budget has not served the public well. In other words, we have significant needs in society around poverty, education, medicine, climate change, etc. When nonprofits don't invest in their teams, solutions that can eradicate social issues around, say, poverty goes unanswered for the public and people in need. Why? There simply is too much to do, and professional learning, innovation, and creativity take time and money.

Overall, a mind shift has to occur. The public understands that it takes money to make a profit in business. People do not have an issue with en-trepreneurs investing in companies, and in fact, American society rewards entrepreneurs. However, nonprofit leaders must educate donors and board members on why the shoestring mentality does not work in the nonprofit sector. We're missing countless opportunities and losing talented people who could make all the difference in ensuring that at least some nonprofits close their doors forever—because a solution made their work no longer necessary.

That said, it takes courage to push back against supporters and board members who challenge nonprofit leaders on managing expenses. Still, I think with the rise of social enterprises and for-profit businesses embracing programs for social good, fearful nonprofit leaders make a significant mistake by not working to shift the thinking of their donors, supporters, and the public. Ultimately, and ironically, we are beginning to see peeling off of fundraising support going from the nonprofit sector to social enterprises, for instance, or direct giving with the rise of new ideas and technologies.

charity: water Goes Against the Grain

In 2019, it became public that the nonprofit charity: water went against the stream, again. If you work in the nonprofit sector, then the chances are high you've heard about the organization whose mission is to ensure that everyone on the planet has clean drinking water access. Since its founding, and as of this book's writing, more than 51,000 water projects have been funding. In 28 countries, more than 11 million people have received access to clean water.

Some years ago, there was a great debate in the nonprofit sector about the market positioning they had done, which went against the grain. At the time, there was a lot of back and forth debate about the fact that charity: water suggested that 100 percent of every donation went directly to programs. Many nonprofit leaders got angry because we all know there are operating costs for any type of organization. However, the reality is that it was much ado about nothing because the nonprofit created a fund called "The Well." A small group of supporters decided to provide investments of five to six figures covering operating costs.

The idea of The Well is brilliant. By separating, with a fund, the nonprofit's operating costs, smaller dollar donors who contribute to charity: water gave 100 percent of their donations to the program costs. I don't see any problem or issue with this approach. It's not disingenuous. It's creative, and, at the time, the plan was innovative. I wonder why more nonprofit leaders haven't followed suit seeking to have a group of supporters cover their nonprofits' operating costs.

However, a nonprofit like charity: water, which seems to be unconcerned by any pushback, and wholly focused on getting the job done, has continued to innovate. Again, people have pushed back on their latest approach, but they keep moving forward—ignoring the critics—and focused on ensuring water for everyone on the planet.

In 2019, *The New York Times*[46] reported that charity:water was at it again. This time around, it was dealing head-on with the issue of pay for its team. The organization understands the problems that affect people in the nonprofit sector. In a world where people can make a lot of money in private industry, they decided to do things differently. Scott Harrison, the CEO, considered nonprofit pay. Harrison has been masterful in creating and maintaining relationships with leading tech companies. Those relationships have helped crystalize for him the reality that people working at charity: water were not earning the wages and bonuses they could command in the for-profit sector. However, ensuring access to clean water for people is an essential mission that requires the best and most creative thinking.

Ultimately, another fund got set up to ensure that charity: water could maintain the best and brightest. This time around, "The Pool" was set up. The following is what is currently on the charity: water website about The Pool.

---

46 A Charity Accepts Uber Stock as Donations. Then Uses It to Pay Staff Bonuses. Is That O.K.?" David Gelles, The New York Times, April 11, 2019, https://www.nytimes.com/2019/04/11/business/charity-water-employees-payment.html?smid=nytcore-ios-share&login=email&auth=login-email

The Pool is a community of business leaders, founders, and entrepreneurs who donate a portion of their private holdings to support our operations and provide a unique employee benefit.

This new program is the first to use proceeds from IPOs and other liquidity events to retain and reward nonprofit employees. It is also the latest way to power our 100% model so that all public donations can go directly to providing clean water for people in need.

In those few words, you see several innovations. First, you have for-private companies committing to share their rewards from a liquidity event with the team from charity: water. Second, Harrison created a unique opportunity for his employees to get rewarded—financially—understanding that they have chosen to work at the nonprofit and not earn the top for-profit salaries they could command.

The "unique employee benefit" referenced is the fact that when for-profit companies, such as Uber, WE, Casper, and Human Ventures, have liquidity events, they've committed to sharing those financial rewards with the team at charity: water. So, members of The Pool transfer or pledge a portion of their financial holdings (approximately 1 percent shares) to the nonprofit, charity: water. When there is a liquidity event, such as an IPO where the sale of shares occurs, money goes to charity: water. 80 percent of the committed proceeds continue to support the nonprofit's 100% model. The remaining 20 percent of the funds go to bonuses for eligible employees of charity: water.

Neil Parikh, Co-Founder, Casper, who pledged to The Pool, said in *The Times* article referring to the charity: water employees, *"They're making below-market salaries. In this tech boom... why should they get left behind? It's a win-win."*

So, my question to nonprofit leaders is this: why aren't innovative solutions like this happening more in the nonprofit sector? Why aren't nonprofit leaders doing what Harrison has done to make the strong case that there is an excellent value to the work completed by their nonprofit team members? The sort of thinking engendered by Harrison across the sector would help ensure that more nonprofits innovate and scale the work they're doing.

Having spoken to thousands of major donors, I believe there's a tremendous opportunity for nonprofit executives to do what Harrison has done. When leaders present a cogent, concise, and compelling case as to why there has to be an investment in the operations, including salaries, I believe donors can and will support those efforts.

However, what donors will not do is invest in nonprofits that keep churning the same old approach to everything. As older donors move on and younger donors—with different ideas, experiences, and sensibilities—enter in more significant numbers to support social good work, their voices will continue to grow. The sound will become louder, demanding that nonprofits get out of the way if they can't create smart, savvy, and innovative solutions.

Doing the Right Thing

It's easy for nonprofit leaders to suggest that they simply don't have the funds to pay their teams a competitive salary. I mean that it's the comfort zone of many leaders in the sector. However, we have to do the right thing and do better. In short, it's a matter of justice and fairness. As a sector, we can't continue to operate with the vast majority of nonprofits simply surviving, duplicating efforts, and making little bits of impact.

In my view, the first place to start making the shift for investment in nonprofit professionals is with nonprofit teams. It doesn't matter if you run a one-person office or you have a large group of people. The nonprofit leader is the first person responsible for ensuring that nonprofit salaries are competitive and not below what is sustainable for people.

That means that nonprofit executives have to change the mentality first within themselves. They have to understand and believe that ensuring nonprofit operations are sustainable is necessary. It is only in coming to terms with it, as Harrison did at charity: water, that organizations could move forward as a sector. That shift in thinking requires a lot of research and introspection.

Making this mental shift can only be done by each nonprofit leader looking in the mirror. It requires commitment, knowledge, understanding, and communication. Nonprofit leaders have to realize that the ball is in their court, and as meaningful changes occur in the industry (and society as a whole), they can continue to tread water or rise and go with the changing flows.

Nonprofits Can Pay Reasonable Salaries

As I mentioned earlier, one of the fail-safes for nonprofit leaders is that they have to be careful paying salaries because of the IRS and also the

AFP. This narrative is convenient, and it is inaccurate to suggest that the IRS does not allow for reasonable wages. The IRS does allow nonprofits to pay "reasonable compensation." It is disingenuous to suggest subtly and between the lines, particularly to young people or others who don't have a lot of experience or work knowledge, that the IRS is the bogeyman and state regulations prevent competitive salaries. They do not. The AFP should look within itself and see what they have supported, I am sure unintentionally, concerning nonprofit compensation.

Operations and Salaries are Vital for the Work
As an industry, we must move away from getting to the lowest common denominator, as it concerns a nonprofit's expenses. It's absurd to operate what is essentially a business and not make any negligible investment. Passion does not pay the bills. While it's an excellent notion, it hurts the industry if it's associated with the idea that you seek to have zero expenses.

Instead, innovative solutions, such as charity: water's funds, The Well, and The Pool, should be at the top of operational thinking. That means that donors and the public have to be informed—consistently—that it takes money to make a difference, or as I mentioned, in time, they will simply support other approaches that are well-resourced. As we all know, investment money is required to test innovative solutions, technology (essential), hire and retain excellent talent.

Humans Matter
One of the best, although there are plenty of others, posts about nonprofit salary and its effect on human lives (i.e., workers) on Nonprofit AF.[47] The following are some of the highlights from that seminal post:

> *...society has the wacky and damaging notion that nonprofit staff should martyr ourselves. It's perfectly OK for celebrities, athletes, and CEOs of companies producing soft drinks or gory video games or yoga pants to be paid millions, but God forbid anyone pay a nonprofit professional 100K to help end homelessness or cancer or whatever.*
>
> *Our sector is sustained by idealists who chose to do this work, who will work for much lower salaries than they could get elsewhere. Young people, especially, who for a*

47 "All right, we need to talk about nonprofit salaries," Nonprofit AF, September 2014, https://nonprofitwithballs.com/2014/09/all-right-you-guys-we-need-to-talk-about-nonprofit-salaries/

while can exist with a small salary, subsisting on ramen and leftover water crackers from community events. I was there. It was kind of romantic, like being a starving artist or a small business owner who makes organic artisanal pickles. But then we do-gooders get older and start thinking about having a family. We start pining for things like a decent used car with brakes and mufflers that actually work.

Further, a follow-up article from Nonprofit AF[48] brought home who poor nonprofit salaries affect. Those individuals are women, families, the young, and people of color. In other words, paying low salaries *harms* nonprofit workers.

Moreover, when we discuss even more sharply issues of race, gender, and social justice, nonprofit compensation has to get addressed. That alone is a reason why nonprofit leaders have to communicate to donors, board members, and the public that this nonsense has to stop.

Tools for Compensation

Finally, once nonprofit executives realize that they have to lead within their organizations, some tools are available to ensure fair and equitable compensation for *all* nonprofit team members. Again, not educating donors and the public about what it takes to make a difference in society is a serious mistake. It opens up the space that should be traditionally for nonprofits—social good—to other ideas and players who can argue that they could make a social impact because they have the resources to do it systematically and at scale. Let's face it; people want to be part of a winning team.

Therefore, it behooves nonprofit leaders to show equity, fairness, and leadership. Compensation is probably the one place where nonprofit executives could lead and show donors, supporters, and the public something before moving on to find other vehicles, ideas, and ways to support their favorite causes.

To be a nonprofit leader for compensation, first, educate yourself on the cost of living. Salary.com has a cost of living calculator that could help you and also your team members. Second, you can understand the laws—and inform your team—about overtime laws in your state. Finally,

---

48 "When you don't disclose salary range on a job posting, a unicorn loses its wings," Nonprofit AF, June 2015, https://nonprofitaf.com/2015/06/when-you-dont-disclose-salary-range-on-a-job-posting-a-unicorn-loses-its-wings/

if you have the funds to hire a compensation expert, do it. It's an excellent investment, which you can do in collaboration with your board and major donors. Also, you can look at some of the top compensation studies in the nonprofit sector. The Bridgespan Group has published an excellent list[49] of places where you can find compensation studies. The National Council of Nonprofits also has a list of compensation resources.[50] However, a simple internet search can provide other excellent resources. What's more important is that nonprofit leaders, donors, and the public believe that is enough is enough.

---

49 "Compensation Resources," The Bridgespan Group, https://www.bridgespan.org/insights/library/careers/selected-compensation-resources

50 "Compensation for Nonprofit Resources, National Council of Nonprofits, https://www.councilofnonprofits.org/tools-resources/compensation-nonprofit-employees

EIGHT

NONPROFIT LEVERAGE THROUGH MERGERS, COLLABORATIONS, AND CONSOLIDATION

"What counts in life is not the mere fact that we have lived. It is what difference we have made to the lives of others that will determine the significance of the life we lead." — Nelson Mandela

On October 19, 1987, I started a nonprofit sector journey for the greater good, leaving behind a law career. My first week as a fundraiser began on Black Monday when the DJIA lost almost 22 percent in a single day, triggering a decline in the global stock market. I took a job as part of an Advancement Team at the University of Notre Dame to raise $350,000,000 for one of its major capital campaigns. The financial world took a breath for a moment, but the market recovered in the coming years. The University exceeded its goal (by $100,000,000) and has surpassed its goals ever since.

I didn't know much about the nonprofit sector and how people thought about giving, but I learned quickly. People and human behavior haven't changed much since, but how people give and their questions have changed. In 1987, there were over 400,000 registered charities in the United States. Estimates for 2020 are approximately 1.6 million charities are now registered with the IRS. In other words, the sector has experienced considerable growth and competition for the charitable dollar.

A single example of the scope and profitability of assisting nonprofits in managing data and fundraising activities in the U.S. is the publicly traded company Blackbaud. Its non-GAAP revenue for 2019 was $880 million to $910 million. This activity, including direct mail, web site development, social media, direct marketing, event planning, staffing, demonstrates the number of resources needed to attract funds for charities.

Giving USA 2019 reported that donors gave $427 .71 billion to charity in the United States. Those numbers also reflect dollars sent to Donor-Advised Funds (DAFs). The billions of dollars going into DAFs have not gotten matched by the outflow of dollars going to fund charities' missions. More money flows from individuals and foundations toward social good, but is it making the impact that it could if there was consolidation in the sector and deployment of resources to solve critical problems? Specifically, for purposes of this chapter is a consideration of solving charities competing against each other for resources from individual donors.

I've long said that all the money in the world exists to solve all the world's problems. As you can see from the information above, resources don't necessarily go to the end user but are either parked assets (assets under management) for future good or fundraise for nonprofit charities. Nevertheless, everywhere I go in the United States, I meet someone who has contributed to philanthropy because something in their heart drives them to make this world a better place.

Marketplace Duplication

I was recently at a gathering of marketplace leaders and religious ministry partners to learn about the issues they are trying to address. Each ministry present had 10 minutes to tell its story, which ended in the need to fund the mission. Most executives did not get into their work for the greater good with any clarity or discussion on raising money.

They have a heart for their work, but most lack the expertise and desire to fundraise. Many are still talking to the same donor groups and essentially competing against each other to provide the same services. That said, the duplication of efforts and lack of knowledge regarding the good practices for raising funds is not limited to religious groups. The same holds for non-sectarian nonprofits.

In every city in this country, I meet people trying to address issues such as human trafficking, poverty, housing, education, homelessness, food insecurity, and a myriad of other activities. Unfortunately, most of these nonprofits are under-resourced and spend a great deal of time raising financial support to further their missions.

However, little time gets spent on taking a look at each city's activities and seeing where there is a duplication of services. A fundamental question that has to get asked is how local charities could work together? Often, donors wonder what programs could get consolidated among nonprofits to optimize and grow services to scale. However, consolidations could happen in other areas such as human resources, legal, accounting, fundraising, or shared office space. In short, there is a lack of much-needed concentration and collaboration in the sector.

Let me give you an example of where consolidation has worked. Several years ago, I met a young man whose mother had passed from colon cancer. He was a musician, but the tragedy in his life impacted him so much that he decided to put his life's work into finding a solution to colon cancer.

Without any real business acumen, he was able to bring the charity to an annual operating budget of $2.5 million. The biggest challenge, however, was meeting payroll monthly. Across town in Washington, DC, was another colon cancer nonprofit with an annual operating budget of $5million. Eventually, the boards met, and over two years, they merged. Today that one charity is the largest colon cancer charity in the country with over $10,000,000 in annual revenue and a unified front.

What I typically see, however, are multiple services provided in the same community. I recently received a call from a board member on a crisis pregnancy center in a large city in the U.S. He was on the board of a client of ours, where we were raising $150 million in a capital campaign.

Knowing of my experience with raising money, he wanted to know how to deal with the multiple requests he received from these charities. Once the charities knew he was pro-life, they all began to approach him. I suggested he bring all the charities together and talk about consulting services. It was too daunting of a task to undertake, as the charities compete with each other for support and covet their donors. In other words, they were not willing to give up an inch of what they viewed as their territories and assets, even if it meant leveraged and improved services for the community.

Unfortunately, many nonprofits work in silos and feel that they have the optimum opportunity for success. From the outside, many professionals in the nonprofit sector and donors believe a lot more could be done for social good if nonprofits formed alliances and potentially even merged. Consequently, organizations' refusal to see beyond their group dilutes the use of charitable dollars and strains the major gift donors in the community. It seems that the same names continually show up in communities of those individuals who could help make a difference. There's a reason for it; competing nonprofits are reaching out to them.

Consolidation in the Past

These are my observations, having been working with charities for the last 30 years. Consolidation was the name of the game for businesses from the mid to late 1980s. I believe that at the same time, the nonprofit sector continued to grow and was unaffected by what was going on in the business marketplace. Now we're at a time where the competition for charitable dollars is fierce, and there is an absolute need for a unified front, especially with faith-based charities.

Further, in a post-pandemic landscape, donors are much more likely to value collaboration and eschew duplication. Nonprofits that understand this time as an opportunity have a higher chance to excite donors at a time of technological innovation, modernity, and continuous disruption.

An example is the competitive marketplace for health care charities that focus on diseases. The quest for charitable dollars places charities against each other. Nonprofits have to understand that traditionally, there are three ways to fund the mission:

1. You dominate in fundraising.
2. You find new donors.
3. You take away market share from other charities.

While competition is useful in making profits for businesses, the social good sector should use additional impact metrics. By aligning and merging, nonprofits can gain efficiencies and expand their work and impact in their communities.

The two simple examples I noted demonstrate the competitiveness for raising money in today's marketplace. To have a greater impact in the communities we serve, nonprofits must consider mergers and consolidation as a means of future survival. It will require people to get in a room together and make some hard decisions about leadership, donor integrity, and shared resources. Several communities I've visited recently have gathered nonprofits in a shared space for conference room usage, shared technology resources, and in some cases, personnel. In turn, the collaborations have maximized the impact of the donors' charitable gifts.

There have been ongoing discussions for years about the need for mergers and consolidation. Jay Love posted on the Bloomerang blog, *"Four Reasons Why More Nonprofits Should Consolidate,"*[51] and they all are sound. Keep in mind that mergers and consolidation are two different legal transactions. His rationale seems to be consistent.

---

51 "4 More Reasons Why More Nonprofits Should Consolidate," Jay Love, Bloomerang, June 8, 2015, https://bloomerang.co/blog/4-reasons-why-more-nonprofits-should-consolidate/

1. Economies of scale. There can be tremendous savings since the charities work for an external good and not an internal profit goal.

2. Overlapping mission. Combining forces may allow some non-profits to operate more efficiently.

3. More efficient fundraising. Donors get stretched by numerous requests from local community charities. My opinion is that you will see more funds set up by donors to help collectively. What the charities don't do the donors will cause them to do

4. New leadership possibilities. This will allow the best to emerge, create new opportunities for committees, and pruning any stagnant activities.

In a published article about nonprofit mergers, one conclusion was as follows:[52]

> *In some ways, it's little wonder that mergers have so few champions within the nonprofit community. They are often associated with leadership failure, financial distress, and good intentions run amok. And experience tells us that nonprofit boards have difficulty discussing mergers. Whether they are unfamiliar with mergers as a restructuring tool or consider merger a last resort, boards generally do not think proactively about mergers or merging.*

It was an interesting study they conducted, as they examined not only completed mergers but also uncompleted and dissolved mergers. Their findings were as follows:[53]

> *To our minds, our most important finding was that in 88 percent of the cases we studied, both acquired and the acquiring nonprofits reported that their organization was better off after the merger, with "better" being defined in terms of achieving organizational goals and increasing collective impact. To be sure, we uncovered the buyer's remorse*

52 Why Emotion Can Derail a Nonprofit Merger," AMA Marketing News, March 1, 2018, https://medium.com/ama-marketing-news/why-emotion-can-derail-a-nonprofit-merger-bb903c7f043c

53 "Nonprofit Mergers That Work," Donald Haider, Stanford Social Innovation Review, March 2, 2017, https://ssir.org/articles/entry/nonprofit_mergers_that_work

and founder regret among merger participants. In the vast majority of cases, however, the participants reported that the merger resulted in increased impact—the critical measure of merger success.

Other findings included the following:

- *In 80 percent of our cases, a prior collaboration existed between the merging organizations;*

- *In 80 percent of the cases, the merging parties engaged a third-party consultant or facilitator;*

- *In 85 percent of the cases, the board chair or a board member from one of the organizations emerged as the chief merger advocate;*

- *In 60 percent of the cases, the acquired organization initiated the merger discussion.*

Mergers Post COVID-19 & The Economic Challenges

Catastrophic events like hurricanes, wildfires, floods have had a devastating impact on some local charities. As we have seen, the world faced a pandemic that had devastating economic consequences for millions, if not billions, of families and people.

As with many small businesses, some charities never return after massively disruptive events. Nevertheless, a lot of this could be avoided with long-term thinking. For instance, COVID-19 reignited the desire for many to drive to support charities on the brink. Once the emergency for dollars diminishes, a lot more thought will happen around strategic alignments and mergers.

One project that I'm incredibly excited about working on today brings together donors from around the country to talk about the things that matter most to them for a collective impact. As you know, my thinking is that donors drive change. The pandemic and economic hit to the economy made people think about ensuring nonprofit programs could get better leveraged to aid communities. Unfortunately, these discussions continue to happen amid great social strife and in the face of a health crisis. Still, they are happening, and as we have seen through history, often massively disrupted events serve as the impetus for change.

Since nonprofits are slow to take advantage of pooling resources, consolidating, merging, and acquiring other nonprofits, the donors will create a scenario where that solution will be the best for the community. Today in New York, for example, a charity brings donors together to learn about topics such as artificial intelligence, blockchain philanthropy, homelessness, education, movie production issues, and impact investing, to name a few.

When donors gather in a collaborative environment to hear what is going on in the community, we find that generosity increases. They see the nonprofit resource and impact problem as twofold. The first challenge is the need for consolidation in the marketplace. Second is the need to bring donors together to work collaboratively in solving some of our communities' most significant challenges.

I desire to work intently with leaders around the country to help promote the change that is needed. For too long, charities have continued to do business as usual. The fundraising climate has changed dramatically in the last few years, and without a look to the future, it will become even harder to survive, especially if there is a market downturn. The most recent example is how devastating COVID-19 was to the nonprofit sector and how short-sighted financial long-term sustainability planning was within charities.

According to the summary of a study on the impact of the pandemic in an article in Candid,[54]

- *In our median baseline scenario, we found that **12,042** nonprofits (4%) would close in the absence of a crisis.*

- *Across nine "realistic" scenarios, a median of **34,472** nonprofits (11%) go out of business.*

- *In this median case, about **22,000** additional nonprofits (7%) close because of the COVID-19 crisis.*

- *In our most optimistic scenario, only **8,420** nonprofits (3%) shut their doors.*

- *In our most dire scenario, we lose **119,517** nonprofits (38%).*

As people get vaccinated, and the pandemic's trauma recedes into history, more nonprofits are taking a reflective look at how they operate. Do-

---

54 "How many nonprofits will shut their doors?" Jacob Harold, Candid, July 15, 2020, https://blog.candid.org/post/how-many-nonprofits-will-shut-their-doors/

nors, board volunteers, and even nonprofit executives will not want to go through their organizations' economic meltdowns again.

In turn, discussions that have already started will only take on more urgency to ensure that communities get served well by the nonprofits in their towns and cities. Inevitably, the conversations and donor dollars will turn to the organizations that realize they can do more, better, and more efficiently by collaborating or even consolidating with other nonprofits.

NINE

DIASPORA GIVING & THE IMMIGRANT NATION

"Let us remember: One book, one pen, one child, and one teacher can change the world." — Malala Yousafzai

Except for the Native American tribes on the land, before we became the United States, all of us come from immigrant families. The idea that our ancestors came from around the world offers us an excellent opportunity to do good, not only within our borders but also outside of it.

As an example, I'm a Brooklyn-bred guy of Italian descent. There were two massive waves of immigration to the U.S. of Italians. The first significant emigration of Italians from its shores started around 1880 and generally ended as fascism rose in Italy. After the Second World War, another substantial amount of migration followed with Italians' exodus to the U.S. In total, about 30 million Italians left the old country for the dream of America.

With that, emigration came the old traditions through families that got passed down from one generation to the next. To this day, many families have customs they follow, gifted to them by their parents, grandparents, great-grandparents, and perhaps even older generations. As a result, ideas and traditions started ages ago continue with a new generation living in the U.S.

For me, it's a connection to Italy. For others, it may be Ireland, China, the Dominican Republic, Colombia, Kenya, Mexico, or South Africa. It doesn't matter where on the planet your family originated from—it's from someplace. Meaning, there is a relationship that extends generations from your family's ancestral country to you in the U.S.

I guess at this point you're wondering, well, how does that relate to philanthropy? My answer is that there's something called diaspora giving. Because of the tools, ideas, and technology we have today, it stands to reason that people from our country may seek to look back to the countries where their families came from and support causes overseas. Also, with the estimated 8 million Americans abroad, they too look back to the land of their birth, the United States, and where they may still have family and friends and decide to contribute to causes from the new places where they live.

For this book, we'll focus on diaspora giving—without including the millions or billions of dollars sent back to home countries in remittances from people who have moved to new countries. Those remittances go back to pay for the essentials and basic needs of families left behind. In other cases, such as with Jewish people giving to Israel, the approximate $3 billion goes to many Israeli needs through government programs. While the reality is that if we were to explore those remittances, they would be a substantial part of diaspora giving, that's not the focus of this book.

Still, nonprofit leaders need to realize an enormous opportunity to tap into new revenue streams exists with diaspora giving. For example, let's say that you happen to run an after-school arts nonprofit program. From the curriculum you and your team have developed, you decide to do a series on Italian art. Thinking of approaching supporters in a way that reminds them of their family roots is an opportunity for more funding.

As I've been saying through this book, donors dictate with their money what they want to prioritize. Diaspora giving affords donors worldwide to support causes and people in the countries where they have roots. As an example, blockchain, which we explored in earlier in the book, can offer donors an opportunity to help people in other places where they have a familial connection. Let's face it, humans need to feel connected, and what better than a place where they think of a historical and familial relationship?

There seems to be nothing better than a link to where peoples' families came, which is why we find companies such as Ancestry, 23and-Me, and others doing so well. People are curious, and they care about their roots, even if it's in another nation. Once they know the village in a foreign country where their family came from, people who are philanthropically minded and have the means may want to support people there as well. Meaning, there is a strong attraction—be it cultural, religious, historical— to understand one's roots. Once people understand their family's history, they get attracted to it, and when they hear stories of need, it's easy for them to leap from supporting a cause in our country to supporting one overseas. Technology, of course, is making it much easier to do it in a globalized digital world.

The Future Meets the Past

For decades, people have understood that globalization was good. Of course, nothing is ever perfect, and while globalization brought with it benefits such as international trade, increased wealth, and better products and services, it also had downsides. Some of the negatives we've seen are that the global elite made a lot more money while the rest of the planet and the poor did not benefit to the degree the elite did.

As we know, amid the pandemic and economic challenges, the elite made money, while millions of Americans lost their jobs. We've also discovered how easy it was to see jobs in America get transferred to lower-wage countries, which is one reason why manufacturing and agricultural industries suffered in the U.S. Naturally, there is now the inevitable reaction away from globalization.

However, the genie is out of the bottle. The global public may want governments to focus on their respective countries and their people. Nevertheless, the fact that the genetic industry continues to grow demonstrates that the world's public interest has not waned. It's just gotten redirected with a sharper focus on individuals instead of whole populations. The curious nature of the human spirit and advances in technology converged to ensure market growth in the U.S. and around the world of ancestral research.

In the U.S., the genetic testing market is valued at $2.43 billion in 2018 and expects to reach $5.05 billion by 2026.[55] This interest in the past was creating fields such as forensic genealogy. It allowed people to learn about their ancestors and their risk factors for diseases such as breast cancer, Type 2 Diabetes, or other conditions. Again, humans always strive to learn about themselves. Now with technology, they can learn not only about their ancestors but also about their medical future.

Because of the convergence of human curiosity and technology, we now have a growing industry, heritage travel, that's bound to take off like never before because of technology. It starts with people placing saliva into a little tube, sending it to a private corporation for processing, getting the results, and getting excited. For some, the journey might end there, but for many others, it is the start of a path to other countries and locations where they have a family history.

---

55 "Direct-To-Consumer (DTC) Genetic Testing Market 2020 Brief Analysis by Top Companies-23andMe, Ancestry, Karmagenes, Color, Genesis HealthCare," Dagoretti News, January 19, 2020, https://dagorettinews.com/direct-to-consumer-dtc-genetic-testing-market-2020-brief-analysis-by-top-companies-23andme-ancestry-karmagenes-color-genesis-healthcare/

Soon, if it doesn't already exist, we'll see on Facebook pages, Instagram, or Twitter stories people sharing their heritage travels. That will only create more demand to look to the past from the present and future lens. Ultimately, for those who are socially minded, it ties back to philanthropy.

You don't think so?

Allow me to draw your attention to a recent *Boston Magazine* article[56] on heritage travel. The author, Abby Bielagus, writes as one of the ten rules for heritage travel to, *"Give Back: Asking your travel guide to arrange a volunteering activity with a local organization is a good way to leave a little bit of yourself behind in the place that made you who you are."* It's just another example of how human nature longs for a connection, even with its family past, once it knows where to look.

As I hope you can see, those same ideas for connection, history, attachment to culture, family, or religion, becomes a path for social good and giving for some people.

Giving Across Borders

We know the internet and social media allow philanthropists to lead efforts that help people. For example, one of my good friends is Wayne Elsey. You may have heard of him because of his incredible efforts to make a difference with shoes. If you don't know the story, here's a short synopsis.

During the holidays of 2004, he was with his family. As the world knows, on December 26, 2004, a 9.1 magnitude earthquake shook the Indian Ocean. That earthquake caused a series of tsunami waves reaching as high as 100 feet. Those waves headed to shore and killed 227,898 people. The disaster was so massive, and the world saw images of utter devastation on their television sets. At the time, it was said that never had so many seen so much suffering and destruction.

When that happened, Wayne was the president of a shoe manufacturing company. Having been in the shoe business since he was 15-year-olds, the way he tells his story is that something inside of him said that he had to do something. Wayne understood that with so much death and destruction, one of the things people would be dealing with was a disease. You have to remember that in many places, people were left with nothing—absolutely no material items, including homes, clothes, or shoes—and they would have to walk to begin to rebuild their lives. However, walking barefoot can cause diseases and could bring more heartbreak.

---

56 "The 10 Commandments of Heritage Travel," Abby Bielagus, Boston News, January 14, 2020, https://www.bostonmagazine.com/travel/2020/01/14/heritage-travel-commandments/

Ultimately, Wayne led efforts to ship more than 250,000 shoes by dialing up other shoe business executives. However, that first experience in social good did not end there. Over the years, Wayne founded one of the fastest-growing nonprofits in the U.S. called Souls4Souls. Since he left that organization, he now oversees several social enterprises under the Funds2Orgs Group, helping nonprofits, schools, families, businesses, and sports teams to raise money with—what else—shoes and sneakers. Those social enterprises also help the planet and its people by keeping gently worn, used, and new shoes and sneakers out of the trash. Ultimately the footwear gets shipped to people worldwide who help themselves out of poverty with work opportunities selling the shoes and sneakers in their local communities.

After the Indian Ocean natural disaster, other natural emergencies followed, such as the earthquakes in Haiti and Puerto Rico, and, more recently, the wildfires in Australia. However, since Wayne first launched his international charitable efforts to the 14 countries affected by the 2004 calamity, global philanthropic efforts have evolved significantly. Since those days, it's become easy to send money around the world—instantly. It started with platforms such as PayPal, but now there are many tools for people to support causes and send money to their ancestral countries or places in need.

Diaspora giving in the 2020s is easy, and evolving innovations make it easier than ever for someone to get to know a place—even remotely—and then support a cause. As an example, Greece faced a debt crisis after the market crash of 2008. In the ensuing years, it put twelve tax increases in place and slashed spending. Also, to stay afloat, the country received bailouts from the European Central Bank, Eurogroup, and the International Monetary Fund. By 2015, riots, protests, and misery were part of the Greek existence.

Greeks who left their country many years ago for the United States witnessed all of what was happening with resolve to help. In other words, they never forgot their homeland. People who returned to Greece during the height of the debt crisis years shared their experiences with others in the U.S., and special funds got created to help support families and orphanages, which was a rarity in Greece. Some years later, when Syrian refugees landed en masse on Greek shores of the bankrupt nation, another round of diaspora giving took place. Greek nonprofits connected to the United States reached out to their fellow countrymen and women to ask for financial support.

The pull of one's heritage can be great, which is why I expect diaspora giving, which is not a new idea or concept, to grow. Technology makes giving to heritage countries easier. As a result, the public is getting back to basics and in philanthropy, seeking to support causes in their ancestral land and new donor vehicles through impact investing funds and blockchain.

Finally, the deep interest in genealogy only leads me to think there will be increased opportunities for nonprofits and diaspora giving. While giving back to the old country has been traditionally more familiar with new immigrants, technology allows new generations or those far removed from their past ancestors to create cultural and heritage connections with other countries aside from the one where they reside.

The Ease of Movement

Diaspora giving, however, goes beyond technology and cultural connections to certain places. For nonprofit leaders and donors to understand how to take advantage of it, they should also know why it plays a significant role. CAF America reported the following:[57]

> One driving force behind the global increase in diaspora giving is the relative ease with which highly skilled workers and talented entrepreneurs now move about in the worldwide community. Increasingly, nations have been willing to facilitate the immigration of hugely successful individuals to foster economic progress. It has resulted in the steady growth of wealthy diaspora populations, which leads to more cross-border gifts. A second motivating factor is the relative ubiquity of the internet and email services. In past generations, cross-border communication's problematic nature proved to be an obstacle for many middle and lower-income migrants looking to maintain a strong connection to their original communities. Even if recent immigrants could maintain contact, the relationship would often end in subsequent generations as descendants became more assimilated. Technological progress has made international communication significantly easier, bolstering foreign and domestic NGOs' ability to cultivate relationships with

---

57 "Trends in Diaspora Giving and Global Impact," International and Domestic Donor Advised Funds, CAF America, https://www.cafamerica.org/trends-in-diaspora-giving-and-global-impact/

diaspora communities spread across the globe. However, building and sustaining these relationships is contingent upon harnessing the power of remittances and global giving technology platforms.

Further, what they reported was that financial donations made by expatriate populations amounted to more than three times global aid. Again, technology, worldwide movement, the refocus to one's nation, and ancestral heritage have all lent themselves to the growth of diaspora giving.

International NGOs Reaching Into and Out of the United States

Suppose you happen to live in cities, such as New York, with high concentrations of immigrants. In that case, you might know there are international nonprofit groups with a reach into the U.S. trying to tap people who have an ancestral or cultural connection to another country.

For instance, a friend of mine who is a New Yorker was researching her family's genealogy, which goes back to Ireland. Members of her family left Ireland in the mid-1800s with many others following the potato famine of 1845-1849. At the time, approximately 25 percent of the Irish population died due to disease and starvation. In doing her research, she learned that her grandfather became a member of one of the fraternal orders.

Think of such organizations as the Ancient Order of Hibernians, Catholic Daughters of America, or the Knights of Columbus. I'm sure you've heard of one or all of them. They're organizations that started with expats from home countries looking to bond and remain connected with their shared culture, language, and history. However, the Irish did not corner the market on fraternal organizations. Think of the Jewish Federation, the Hispanic Heritage Foundation, or Aid for Africa. They all seek to tap into people who have a cultural and ancestral connection for continued development and support, in some cases, of causes and people outside of the U.S.

In reverse, American expats overseas are tapped to do good back home. While many people may never be expats in their lives, there is certain psychology and connection in being abroad that many expats experience. Expats often understand that they represent—even in a small way—their home countries. While it's unfair for people to view expats as representative of their passports, humans are still human. It's only natural for people to form a mental idea when they meet an American, Australian, Kenyan, or Indian overseas.

Expatriates often support giving in their home countries because it's a way for them to stay connected with their families, friends, and culture. It's also a way for them to demonstrate to their friends and acquaintances back home that even though they no longer live in their home country, they still care about what happens with the people back home. Because of it, many nonprofits in the U.S. seek to attract expats who live in the country and abroad.

President Jimmy Carter and his wife, Rosalynn, founded The Carter Center in partnership with Emory University. The focus of the nonprofit is its commitment to human rights and alleviating human suffering around the world. Further, its aim is "to prevent and resolve conflicts, enhance freedom and democracy, and improve health." However, although it was founded in the United States by a former American President and First Lady, it accepts donations from all over the world. No matter the location, including many Americans in the U.S. and overseas, its donors support this organization's mission and work.

Many people may not realize this, but Doctors Without Borders is a French nonprofit organization, of which the French are immensely proud. In 1968, a group of physicians in France decided they had to help victims of disasters and war. They created Médecins Sans Frontières (MSF), which is known in English as Doctors Without Borders. During this time, French citizens saw suffering on their television screens by way of a revolt in Southern Nigeria. The images broadcast to the French public included children dying of hunger.

Today, Doctors Without Borders, and the other group that split off from the organization, Doctors of the World (Médecins du Monde) after a disagreement on how to aid refugees in the South China Sea, are leading international nonprofits going into some of the most dangerous situations. Both of these organizations and their medical professionals have stood on their front lines of everything from SARS, the Syrian refugee crisis, to the latest threat, the coronavirus. Both of these organizations have significant support from Europeans, including French, and also Americans.

Trends for Diaspora Philanthropy
While we have shifted to less globalization, we're not going to escape it. You only have to look as far as technology to realize that even if countries want to create hard borders, we're not going back to a place where people in one part of the world had no idea of what was happening on the other side of the planet.

Therefore, I think it's a mistake to believe that diaspora philanthropy has seen its peak. I think we couldn't be further from the truth. Sure, the coronavirus could have tamped the demand, and it may take time to increase, but technology continues to develop unabated. That means that the world continues to become smaller and easy to navigate, even between massive distances.

In a globalized world that is not going back to the past, diaspora giving is only going to continue to grow. It will also go beyond our focus on billionaire and millionaire philanthropists, focusing on any research about international philanthropy. Instead, because of tools and innovative approaches, such as blockchain, or impact investing and ideas that we have not yet gotten created, we're going to see diaspora philanthropy continue to develop. Therefore, I'd like to focus on where I think the world is going with this form of giving.

Distrust Leads to New Routes

At the moment, the American public is going through a massive instance of suspicion, as we all know. Nonprofits need public trust to ensure that they succeed. You would think that people would have a bit more confidence in nonprofits that don't have a profit motive for existing. However, that's not the case. The public also views nonprofits with suspicion, and there's a lot of reason for it.

For instance, nonprofit boards have not been representative of the populations they serve. Also, we know that billionaires pay low-income tax, and then suggest that they give back to society through philanthropy. However, a lot of the money goes to institutions with large endowments (e.g., universities, high-ranking hospitals, museums, etc.).

Unfortunately, many smaller community and social service groups don't receive any attention from people with great wealth. Other reasons include a lack of trust that nonprofit leaders fall within the purview of the organizations themselves, such as suspicion that nonprofits can protect sensitive information (generally speaking, they can't). Often, nonprofits lack transparency, and there are even some where board members care less about the public interest than personal benefits.

In fact, according to the Edelman Trust Barometer, as reported in the article[58] on the Nonprofit Law Blog, *"...the trust percentage in nonprofits dropped from 58 percent in 2017 to 49 percent in 2018 before moving slightly back up to 52 percent in 2019."*

---

58 "Public Trust and Nonprofits: What's Going On?" Gene Takagi, Nonprofit Law Blog, November 7, 2019, http://www.nonprofitlawblog.com/public-trust-and-nonprofits-whats-going-on/

In light of what we've discussed in this book, there are new opportunities for donors and supporters who simply don't trust nonprofits for diaspora philanthropy or giving, for that matter. For instance, as I wrote earlier in the book, nonprofits are not the only organizations focused on social good. Social enterprises and for-profit businesses support people who care about social good, including international work. In the process, they are investing and also obtaining financial returns.

Remittances Help Drive Diaspora Giving

Those of us in the nonprofit sector understand that payments that expats send back home to their relatives cannot be considered diaspora philanthropy. Those two things are separate and distinct. When expats send money back to their home countries, they do it for their families' benefit, which is a kind gesture but cannot be considered philanthropy.

However, *Alliance Magazine* published that in the United Kingdom, at least, there was a strong relationship between remittances and charitable giving. As they reported, *"...households that send or 'remit' money overseas are more likely to make donations to domestic U.K. charities than the general UK population is: 42per cent among remitters, compared with 29per cent of households in the general population."*[59]

It stands to reason. Even though remittances are the transfer of money from people living in poverty to other people living in poverty, when people send payments back home, they demonstrate some of the qualities necessary for philanthropic giving. In other words, they are looking outside of themselves and trying to help improve others' lives. When people send remittances back home, they understand the circumstances in their adopted country (e.g., economy, work opportunities), but they also remain connected to their international community.

More NGOs Partner with American Counterparts

The world understands that for generations, Americans have been the most philanthropically minded individuals on the planet. Sure, a lot of that has come because we've had taxation and laws that have encouraged philanthropy. Also, relative to many parts of the world, Americans are wealthier than people in other countries, especially developing nations.

---

59 "Diaspora philanthropy, giving effectively across borders and emerging trends in global philanthropy," Nicolas Makharashvili, Allianze Magazine, June 2015, https://www.alliancemagazine.org/blog/diaspora-philanthropy-giving-effectively-across-borders-and-emerging-trends-in-global-philanthropy/

As we know, there is poverty in our country, and millions of people go to bed hungry, but generally speaking, as a nation, we're an incredibly wealthy country. With the unrest in our society in 2020, Americans have to work harder to ensure that all citizens have a realistic opportunity at the old and tired American Dream. However, in comparison to millions of people living in other countries, we are a wealthy nation.

Therefore, as the world becomes a much smaller place because of the ease of communication and the power of diaspora, we have a situation in the United States where organizations founded in other countries have reached out to groups in the U.S. to partner with them.

As an example, one of the places to look is concerning climate change. We know that the Trump Presidential administration, thus the federal government, pulled out of the Paris Climate Accord. They did not believe in climate change as human-made, so they do not make any efforts to combat the global crisis. However, as of this writing, President Joe Biden will move us to rejoin.

However, the world understands that the U.S. is an influential nation. Americans need to be involved in the development of solutions to battle the climate crisis. One of the initiatives that got a lot of press was created by former Presidential candidate and billionaire Michael Bloomberg. At present, 25 cities in the U.S. have resolved to do their part to meet the international climate accords by lowering carbon emissions through the American Cities Climate Challenge.

During Giving Tuesday 2019, there was a lot of ink used by publishers and journalists encouraging people around the world to donate to international nonprofit organizations on the front lines of the climate crisis. As an example, this article titled,[60] "*Want to fight climate change effectively? Here's where to donate your money*" by Vox was one of many published. Now, regardless that many people view climate change as an existential threat, only 8 percent of American giving goes toward the effort.[61]

That said, during 2019, one of the beneficiaries of international support was 350.org. The organization promotes international and grassroots giving exceptionally well. They describe themselves as "*an interna-*

---

60 "Want to fight climate change effectively? Here's where to donate your money" Sigal Samuel, Vox, December 18, 2019," https://www.vox.com/future-perfect/2019/12/2/20976180/climate-change-best-charities-effective-philanthropy

61 "These are the favorite charitable causes of the world's wealthiest families — and climate change is NOT one of them," Leslie Albrecht, MarketWatch, January 25, 2020, https://www.marketwatch.com/story/the-1-gives-more-money-to-arts-culture-and-sports-than-to-fighting-climate-change-survey-of-billionaires-finds-2020-01-23

tional movement of ordinary people working to end the age of fossil fuels and build a world of community-led renewable energy for all." In the little more than ten years since university friends in the U.S. founded it, the organization has truly gone global. It is reaching out to expats and the international community for support.

The group's first task was to create a global day of action, including the International Day of Climate Action in 2009, Global Work Party in 2010, and Moving Planet in 2011. Since then, they've demonstrated against the Keystone K.L., and Dakota Access pipelines, worked to stop fracking in Brazil and Argentina, and have partnered with more than 1,000 institutions, cities, and religious groups to divest more than $12 trillion from fossil fuels. In just over a decade, this organization is a global powerhouse fighting climate change and attracting money and activist support from international expats and people in South America, North America, Europe, Africa, Australia, and Asia. In other words, it's a powerhouse for change.

350.org has sought to develop strategic partnerships and what they call "allies" worldwide for their mission. For example, partners include Greenpeace, World Council of Churches, and MoveOn.org.

So, while the United States government has decided that it is not interested in combatting climate change, you have groups reaching into the U.S. and those created by people in the States seeking to address this global threat.

However, global and diaspora giving are not just related to climate change, although that's probably the most straightforward example. You also have fraternal organizations, such as the YMCA, Lions Clubs, Rotary Clubs, and other internationally-based nonprofits that understand how essential it is to keep money coming into their coffers from generous American donors.

In conclusion, international philanthropy is not something that is going to end any time soon. It's just not possible for it to happen at an age where technology has eliminated borders in many ways. Further, as technology aids opportunities for people worldwide to access American donors' generosity, it's only to be expected that more money will be heading to causes that benefit not only Americans but also people in other nations.

TEN

THE 21ST CENTURY DONOR MINDSET

"The meaning of life is to find your gift. The purpose of life is to give it away." — Pablo Picasso

Chris Lyons, President/Publisher, Nonprofit Pro, recently said to me, *"The current and future state of the donor mindset may be at its most transformative and dynamic stage since the dawn of television. Where, when, and how donors are engaged and committed to certain charities closely mirrors the customer experience models of for-profit organizations. Nonprofits must understand and leverage all communication touchpoints to their optimal levels to maximize current contributions and set the foundation for the future."*

One of the consistent themes throughout this book is that donors drive the change needed to have a more significant impact on the communities in which they live. New technologies, ideas, societal sensibilities, and ways of communicating are fundamentally shifting philanthropy as donors seek to leverage their options in varying ways.

Throughout the time I've spent consulting nonprofits, we've addressed diversified revenue streams. Those typically include major gifts, planned giving, campaigns, events, peer to peer, direct mail, annual fund, matching gifts, tithing, to name a few. However, the new models need to include alternative revenue sources and approaches for a new kind of donor who is tech-savvy and much more socially aware of societal changes because of social media, globalization, and the user experience in everything they do with technology.

One such vehicle that we touched upon was impact investing. A generation ago, the nonprofit community was the principal place to find people focused on transforming the world for the better. That's no longer the case, and as Chris mentioned, we see how for-profit ideas and experiences are now infused into philanthropy.

Traditionally, someone who wanted to scale a market solution and earn money would start a business; those who wanted to make a dent in global poverty, transform a local community, or care for widows and orphans began a nonprofit charity. But that's all changed today. That delineation that existed gave way to other ideas and market-based solutions, including social enterprises, impact investing, blockchain, etc.

I believe most nonprofits in the future need to think broadly. Nothing is off the table. For example, nonprofit leaders should ask themselves if the right vehicle for making a difference is a nonprofit. Maybe it is, but perhaps it's not. As artificial intelligence rises, new ways of giving incentivize donors to support a cause and get financial returns. So, maybe it makes sense to create a for-profit social enterprise.

Alternatively, it may be a good idea to create a donor-advised fund for the organization for more immediacy. Fundraisers might want to consider focusing on blockchain as money gets fully digitized. Out of the box, thinking could come in many forms, depending on the organization.

For instance, Habitat for Humanity's ReStores has capitalized on a niche in the marketplace by selling donated products, mostly things aligned with their mission. In other words, they depend not only on donors' philanthropy to give to charity, but they sell merchandise to help support their work. They generate a healthy proportion of their operating budget from activities that allow the charity to be self-sustaining and act more like a business.

The first Habit for Humanity Restore opened in the mid-1980s in Winnipeg, Canada, followed by the first U.S. store in Austin to raise revenue and promote its sustainability message. These stores provide a steady income source for the nonprofit, thus allowing them to have a more significant impact on the communities they serve.

At the 2019 Habitat for Humanity International Conference, Jonathan Reckford, CEO, noted the ReStores generated over $450 million in revenue. Habitat ReStores operated in the United States and five additional countries in 2019. A total of 903 Restores can be found across 49 of the 50 U.S. states, with an extra 130 spread through Canada, New Zealand, Australia, Northern Ireland, and the Philippines.

Another example of creatively thinking out of the traditional nonprofit box is how Opportunity Zones provides economic renewal through tax law. That tax law allows investors to defer paying federal capital gains tax on the property's sale if those gains get invested in a qualified opportunity fund. In turn, those funds get invested in low-income census tracts[62] designated as Opportunity Zones.

This new incentive relies on equity investments rather than traditional debt and subsidy instruments. Foundations and communities are looking at solutions that transcend what traditional philanthropy can address. Private foundations hold over $1 trillion and assets, and these can be used to have a more significant impact in the 8,700 Opportunity Zones across the nation.

What should give us the heart is that donors continue to support social good causes. They just want to do it innovatively with solutions for the 21st Century. My friend, Andrew M. Aran, Managing Partner, Regency Wealth Management, and his wife continue to be committed to social good causes, as so many millions of others are in the world. However, it's crucial to realize that donors will do it on their terms and their way.

Andy commented about his giving, *"My wife's and my perspective are maintaining a steady lifestyle that doesn't rise or fall as our income fluctuates and not overplaying it by trying not to accumulate more than we need. While that is highly subjective, we have decided that we will give away anything over a certain net worth threshold. Years ago, that translated into a tithe or ten percent of our income. In recent years it has been equal to if not surpassed our annual income. Give while you live so that you can see the fruits of your (HIS) generosity is our motto, rather than wait until we die."*

As the Philanthropic World Changes

We've discussed a lot, and it feels as if we've gone all around the world. Since I started writing this book, which has been less than one year, so much has transpired, and I imagine that will be the case for the rest of my life. That said, I want to close this book talking about the donor mindset of the 21st Century donor.

There was a time—when I started my career as a fundraiser—where the world was as it was. Things changed, of course, but they seemed to take a lot longer than they do these days. When I started working as a fundraiser, there was no such thing as social media. Imagine life before Facebook and Instagram—it did exist. A lot of what we use to do as fundraisers would take weeks. For instance, if we wanted to run reports, we would have to walk over to a data manager who would then generate a

---

62 "How Philanthropy Can Ensure Opportunity Zones Ensure Widespread Economic Renewal," Bruce Katz, The Chronicle of Philanthropy, April 25, 2019, https://www.philanthropy.com/article/Opportunity-Zones-Could-Become/246177

report whenever they got around to it.

If we wanted to personalize letters, we would create segmented lists and group people into different segments. Today, that idea seems quaint. Now we have donor fundraising technology that can entirely personalize letters for every person on your database and create thousands of individual messages that are entirely custom and directed to each donor prospect. Back in the day, fundraisers who had to get an appeal out the door by the deadline could easily find themselves late at night at the office licking envelopes.

All of these days are pretty much over. Today, we have technology tools doing a lot of the work fundraisers were doing. I had a recent conversation with someone who has been a fundraiser for many years. Both of us now envision a world where fundraising teams change. With the human and AI partnership, organizations are moving toward relying on powerful artificial intelligence to raise much-needed funds, much more strategically. Copywriters, general gift fundraisers, and grant writers, I can see partnering with AI tools for their work. Of course, everyone should begin to advance their skills because most jobs will transform or disappear in less than a decade.

However, it's not just technology that is a bit of an existential threat to today's nonprofits. It's also donors and the public who don't trust nonprofit leaders and who are, frankly, tired of donating every year and not seeing the ball move much further in a positive direction. They want transparency and results. We understand that we live in a world of "disruption and innovation." If nonprofits are not disrupting and innovating, there's a real threat they're going to be left behind because they will be considered old.

For this chapter, in particular, I asked leaders and donors to give me their take on what they see happening in philanthropy and the future of fundraising as it relates to the donor mindset. Nonprofits have to evolve because they have no choice. Donors are moving with the times, and they will not support causes that don't keep up with the changes to solve the intractable social issues people believe need fixing.

To that end, I connected with a friend and major donor, Ernie Bono. He told me, *"Donors today—large donors—want to know when giving to an endowment, what happens years from now when current leadership is no longer involved and or the charity is not viable? Also, people want more transparency in terms of expenses and how much is going to the cause. Donors want to be updated on how the charity is doing on a year by year basis...I could go on and on. I'm currently raising money...I also find development professionals are not very good."*

I think that last thought from Ernie has to do with the fact that many fundraisers haven't yet absorbed the fact that donors have changed because society has changed. Many fundraisers continue with the mentality that was fine for the 20th Century. But ideas that are more than 20 years old don't make any sense in the 21st Century with so many opportunities for donors to support a good cause in innovative and creative ways.

As Ernie suggested in his comments, fundraisers and nonprofit leaders must be aware of philanthropic changes. Still, some fundraisers do understand what's happening with donors. I'd like to share some of the words a highly-skilled global fundraiser had to say. John Cerniglia, Senior Vice President & Chief Development Officer, U.S.A., and Chief Development Officer, Global for Operation Mobilization, expressed the following when I asked him about the donor mindset.

> *I think this depends on the subsector. For example, in the child welfare space, we see more demand for evidence-based programming that produces predictable outcomes for kids at risk. It's no longer enough to give a kid a free lunch and hope for the best. Philanthropists know better, and demand proved interventions that drive transformational outcomes.*
>
> *Secondly, we see more and more drive for prevention. If your cause is domestic violence or poverty housing, wise donors want to know what you are doing to get in front of the problem and prevent adults and children from ever facing such high levels of toxic stress. It's akin to a local fire department. The more they remind us to have working smoke alarms, the fewer the number of fires they have to run into at a much lower cost.*
>
> *So, donors ask: what are you doing to reduce the levels of domestic violence? What are you doing so when the next tornado strikes, the house remains standing?*
>
> *At Operation Mobilization, where I serve as global C.D.O., our aim is for the gospel of Jesus to be within reach of everyone on the planet. Today, 3 billion people live without seeing the love of Jesus lived out in the life of another. Our donors are looking for gospel integration more than ever. How well are we presenting the full gospel (think Matt 25 and Matt 28) in both word and deed, in a holistic manner? Increasingly, faith-based donors are looking for integration.*

One final note: stewardship. Donors and philanthropists demand measurable results. And well they should! If they entrust us with their money so we can turn and use it for good, we are called to world-class stewardship. I think the parable of the talents is the perfect model. What did the three guys do when the master returned? They reminded the master of what he gave to them (we should remind every donor how much they entrusted to us), then they reported on what they did with the money and the extent to which their use of the money produced fruit. We in the sector should be eager to share what we did with each gift and the fruit we've seen in advance of our mission!

There's a lot of strategic thinking that must occur in the philanthropic sector. Nonprofit leaders cannot rest and think that the past results will mean they will continue to perform in the future. If nothing else, this book should remind you how donors seek new ideas in response to the enormous and continuous changes.

Another major donor and friend, Tony de Nicola, President & Managing Partner, Welsh, Carson, Anderson & Stowe, and who has substantially impacted philanthropic causes throughout the country, shared the following insights from his perspective.

Benefactors today are much more interested in results and outcomes that emanate directly from their gifts. As a benefactor, I want a clear understanding of the societal problem being addressed, the program or solution supported to ameliorate that problem, and tangible metrics agreed in advance to defining success and the actual results achieved. Long gone are the days when major benefactors blindly turn over a meaningful amount of capital to a nonprofit organization without such previously agreed terms.

Related to the topic of defining success at the outset of a major gift is the concept of a well-drafted "gift agreement." For large gifts, sophisticated families and benefactors require specificity in donor gift agreements that will outlast the living participants in the transaction today for decades into the future. These terms are meant to ensure the receiving institution's honor, in perpetuity, the wishes of the

*current benefactor as to how the gift will be used. I have
been involved in drafting several of these gift agreements
for our family with receiving institutions, and it has been a
process to get all the lawyers and principals to understand
the family's intentions and the expectations for the use of
funds. You may think this is not that much of a problem,
but we have actually walked away from a couple of institutions that would not agree to the terms of what we wanted
in our gift agreement. Donors are much more sophisticated
and demanding in this regard, and receiving institutions
will learn to adapt to this new reality.*

*Some gifts we were in discussion to make were ter-
minated early in the negotiations with the receiving institutions because it was clear that an agreement would not be
reached.*

Tony raised a good point here that we did not mention earlier in the book.
The idea that major gift donors are now much more open than they once
were to terminate gift agreements if they feel the objectives are not getting
met.

D.G. Elmore, Chairman, The Elmore Companies, shared his insights as well as a significant philanthropist. If you notice his words, you
see a frustration with fundraisers who do not understand how donors operate in the world of today.

*… I think what most fundraisers miss is THAT they are so
focused on their projects and the organizational goal and
THAT they fail to understand what projects donors are
interested in funding. Sure, one approach is to throw projects on a list to your major donors and then let them say
yes or no as if choosing from a menu, but I DON'T FIND
THAT HELPFUL. A sophisticated and truly socially focused
and Christ-centered fundraiser should be more interested
in discovering the donor's passions and purposes and then
figuring out how to develop initiatives around a collective
mass of donors."*

What these quotes from these leading philanthropists suggest is that fundraisers and nonprofits have to do a much better job of understanding the

contemporary donor. As we know, we live in a modern world that is driven by transparency, authenticity, metrics, creativity, innovation, and disruption. While Millennials and Generation Z grew up with these ideas, you can't dismiss the notion that Gen Xers and Boomers, who are also socially aware, understand that they could demand more of the nonprofits and social good groups they choose to support.

Looking Beyond Old

The public is done with old thinking—and so are donors. I've spoken to more than 4,000 donors during my time as a professional fundraiser. One of the major themes is the constant frustration of things in the nonprofit sector, seemingly not changing.

One of them, Jay M. Ferriero, President & CEO, Capital Automotive, spoke to the evolution of what new donors do not want to experience. He said, *"The next generation is at risk of being less in touch socially as they are tangentially social...mindset needs to adjust as what was once meaningful for this generation is not going to be how they stay in touch in the future. Don't think that going to expensive platted dinners and being at events in person is going to be as meaningful as it once was for nonprofits."*

The pandemic of 2020 pushed nonprofit organizations—by force—into having to innovate because the old (and expensive) dinners did not happen. Perhaps, the silver lining of a tough situation of the pandemic is that it's forced nonprofits across the country to reconsider how they relate to their donors and raise money. Moreover, it will be interesting to see in the coming years if more nonprofits do what they should have done long ago, which is to collaborate, merge, consolidate, or even close if they are not making much of a meaningful impact.

I'm quite surprised that we still have a situation where we have more than 1.6 million nonprofits in the U.S. Those of us in the sector understand that something's got to give. What's more challenging for donors to stomach is the reality that 20.85 percent of nonprofits have budgets of less than $50,000 and 20.69 percent less than $100,000.[63]

Donors understand that there's not a whole lot you can do with a total operating budget of $50,000 or even $100,000. Imagine everything that has to be done on that budget. For instance, unless a nonprofit is volunteer-driven, which many are because they don't have the resources to pay anyone, there's salary and benefits to pay. More than likely, the non-

---

63 "How Big Are Most Nonprofits?" ZipSprout, https://zipsprout.com/how-big-are-most-non-profits/

profit is not operated out of someone's office, and so there's rent, electricity, and operating expenses to cover. One has to presume that a nonprofit has a database and wants to do outreach to get supporters who will bring more money and spread the word. Imagine those costs, and we haven't even talked about the program costs.

It doesn't take a lot of business savvy for donors who realize many nonprofits' dire circumstances to take a pass. Would you want to donate $10 or $100 or more to a nonprofit that may not be operating next month? I wouldn't. People want to support social good causes and organizations that are making an impact. However, few people want to contribute to nonprofits that are not doing much more than treading water.

Another friend and major donor of mine, Henry Kaestner, Co-Founder and Partner, Sovereign's Capital, mentioned to me, *"Two things I'd mention are the emphasis on metrics and also an articulation of the competitive landscape. In my opinion, too many nonprofits talk about the problem they're trying to solve without acknowledging others are working to do the same. A big red flag for me anytime I'm reviewing a plan from an entrepreneur is when they make it sound like they're the only people in the space. Having a comprehensive view of the competitive landscape and then at the same time talking about their key differentiator and what they're uniquely equipped to do is very, very helpful, and shows a thoughtful leader that is focused on the bigger picture."*

Also, there are other vital issues that nonprofits must also address, as I've highlighted in this book. Money and fundraising do play a part in it and how well fundraisers understand the changing and evolved thinking of modern donors. Still, at the risk of repeating myself, I believe other issues are significant challenges (or opportunities depending on how you look at it) for innovative and ambitious nonprofit leaders. First is the technology and data protection in a world increasingly lived online and warehoused in the cloud. Second is the idea of social justice, and for that, I had the input of a talented journalist, philanthropist, and activist.

Protection of Sensitive Data

As I mentioned earlier in the book, donor privacy and security of sensitive information matter, and nonprofits need to heed data security warnings. With the start of the new decade, we had states in the U.S. follow the European's lead concerning data protection. California, Nevada, Washington, New Jersey, and New York have created laws protecting information gathered by businesses and other organizations, such as nonprofits.

I wonder what donors would think if they truly understood how vulnerable their data is at many nonprofit organizations, including their credit card information, Social Security information, and other sensitive data. A few weeks ago, I was speaking to a fundraising consultant, and he mentioned how he created as part of his agreement protection of donor information. He said that as laws evolve and people become more aware of their data and unauthorized use, they do not want the liability.

Still, this fundraising consultant, who works with small to medium-sized nonprofits, regularly gets database exports and Excel files from nonprofit leaders, including names, addresses, giving history, and other sensitive personal information. He said he immediately deletes these emails and purges his data systems of the data. Still, he lamented that although he has explicitly legal language in his contracts that prohibits this type of personal data transfer, nonprofits still do it.

Nonprofits, especially those with limited financial resources, are a prime target for criminal hackers. On top of that, you have well-intentioned but thoughtless nonprofit leaders. They think nothing of sending sensitive donor information via email to consultants or other people they believe should have it. It's a severe and grave mistake, and if donors understood how poorly some nonprofits care for their data, I doubt they would make another charitable donation.

Therefore, nonprofit leaders must understand that one of the most vital responsibilities they have is to protect all of their supporters' data and information. If nonprofit leaders do not prioritize this, candidly, their nonprofit should close its doors. If nonprofits don't prioritize a portion of their contributions to ensuring the integrity of their databases, websites, servers, donation forms, etc., then they shouldn't be in business.

Again, if donors knew and absorbed the reality that so many nonprofits are at risk from hackers and attacks, they would probably stop giving. However, even small nonprofits can get ahead of this reality. At some point, there is going to be a significant nonprofit hack. Unfortunately, it will involve donor information, and it's going to make all of the papers. If it can happen to Equifax and banks, it can happen to any nonprofit. However, even small organizations with limited resources can get ahead of the protection of donor data.

If you think this is not something that donors can know about your nonprofit, you would be wrong. CharityWatch.org works to inform donors about donor privacy policies[64] and protection. Therefore, nonprofits listed on the site have information related to "Governance & Transparency." Further, in their report, Charity Rating Guide & Watchdog Report, they have a symbol after each charity's name denotes a lack of a privacy policy. In other words, the public does care about privacy and data protection, which is why states in the United States have started to change their laws. Expect more to follow.

Social Justice and Philanthropy

While the donors whom I've connected with about the donor mindset have expressed their ideas about how they think, there's one topic that was brought about by my friend, Ponchitta Pierce. Ponchitta is a communications expert who works with her clients to maximize their potential through communications and oral histories.

Ponchitta was also a television host, producer, and journalist. She began her journalism career at Ebony magazine and eventually rose to become the New York Editor and New York Bureau Chief of the magazine's parent company, Johnson Publications. She's also worked at C.B.S. News, WNBC-TV, and W.N.E.T., among her notable career highlights.

She has served in causes for many years and is a member of the board of directors of the Foreign Policy Association; W.N.E.T.; the Inner-City Scholarship Fund of the Catholic Archdiocese of New York; Housing Enterprise for the Less Privileged (H.E.L.P.); and the Cuban Artists Fund. She is also a member of the Council of Foreign Relations, The Economic Club of New York; the Columbia-Presbyterian Health Sciences Advisory Council; and the Advisory Board of the University of Southern California Center on Public Diplomacy.

In connecting with Ponchitta about my book, one of the first things she had to say was that we need to drive home the point here that donors are not looking for the same-old, same-old. They are open to change, experimentation, and are using modern tools and platforms to help move philanthropy.

As we know, in 2020, the United States (along with the world) faced the pandemic, an economic hit of massive job loss as a reaction to stay-at-home orders, for instance, and also social justice protests as a result

---

64 "How To Check If a Charity Respects Your Privacy," October 19, 2018, CharityWatch.org, https://www. charitywatch.org/charity-donating-articles/how-to-check-if-a-charity-respects-your-privacy

of the events following the death of George Floyd. [65] I believe that life is a journey where there is a lot of learning, and I will continue to listen and want to share ideas. In her comments for this book, Ponchitta was able to synthesize everything we face.

Ponchitta acknowledged that the world and our country face *"uncertainty because of the election, COVID-19, and the digital age. Yet, new formations and associations are developing."* As most of us believe, Ponchitta believes that we will never look the same as we did going into the momentous year of 2020.

She alluded to the realities that following the protests following Mr. Floyd's death, a heightened awareness came about social justice issues and race. The truth is that we all know how Colin Kaepernick's career with the N.F.L. came to an end in January of 2017[66] as he protested, in his words, *"... the injustices that are happening in America, the oppression that is happening in America."*

Although, as Ponchitta explained, philanthropic dollars have flowed to causes serving Black communities[67], including the Vanderbilts and Reed Hastings, CEO, Netflix, and his wife, Patty Quillin, giving to historically Black colleges for example, but "it's never been enough." However, awareness about gender, economic, and racial justice has come to the forefront, and younger generations no longer expect talk but action.

Modern-day philanthropists, aside from Hastings and Quillin have stepped up, such as MacKenzie Scott, who reportedly distributed $1.7 billion to 116 organizations since she spoke about her philanthropic intentions since May, 2019.[68] Scott is the former wife of Jeff Bezos, CEO, Amazon. She's moved to support causes aimed to create racial, economic, climate change, and gender equality. Historically Black institutions of education, Howard University and Tuskegee University, said that her gifts

---

65 "How George Floyd Was Killed in Police Custody," Evan Hill, Ainara Tiefenthäler, Evan Hill, Christiaan Triebert, Drew Jordan, Haley Willis and Robin, Stein, The New York Times, May 31, 2020, https: www.nytimes.com/2020/05/3/us/george-floyd-investigation

66 "TIMELINE: Colin Kaepernick's journey from San Francisco 49ers star to kneeling to protest racial injustice," Juan Carlos Guerrero, A.B.C. 7 News, August 26, 2020, https://abc7news.com/colin-kaepernick-kneeling-when-did-first-kneel-date-what-does-do-now/4147237/

67 "Borealis Philanthropy Launches Fund to Advance Racial Equity in Philanthropy," Borealis Philanthropy, August 2, 2018, https://borealisphilanthropy.org/borealis-philanthropy-launches-fund-to-advance-racial-equity-in-philanthropy/

68 "5 takeaways from MacKenzie Scott's $1.7 billion in support for social justice causes," Elizabeth J. Dale, The Conversation, July 30, 2020, https://theconversation.com/5-takeaways-from-mackenzie-scotts-1-7-billion-in-support-for-social-justice-causes-143659

were the largest given to them ever by any individual donor.

It was not until 2020 that it seemed that Corporate America stepped up to meet the moment. For example, Walmart announced that it would give $100 million[69] over the course of five years to create a center for racial equity. However, other companies also announced contributions in support of racial, social justice issues.[70]

Moreover, leading foundations have decided to spend more of the funds they have at their disposal to give, including an emphasis on Black Americans. As Darren Walker, President, Ford Foundation, said of an initiative that closed in 2020, *"We are going to allocate it to institutions working on the front lines for justice in the United States and other parts of the world. Organizations are working on including all Americans in voting; organizations are providing solutions as we think about how to reimagine our law enforcement system. We're going to fund organizations working on the criminal justice system and ending mass incarceration, as well as our national arts and cultural treasures. These organizations are at risk. And if we do business, as usual, we will watch many of them fall off a cliff."*[71]

The effort by the Ford Foundation is a collaborative that also includes John D. and Catherine T. MacArthur Foundation, the W.K. Kellogg Foundation, the Andrew W. Mellon Foundation, and the Doris Duke Charitable Foundation. Together, they plan to contribute $1.7 billion in grants to support social justice issues in the coming years. They are doing this by borrowing $1 billion worth of 30 and 40-year bonds instead of dipping into their immense endowments to take advantage of the historically low-interest rates.

As Ponchitta expressed, the time for dialogue has finished, and it is time for action to improve the lives of what have been historically marginalized communities, including Black Americans, Native Americans, and also Latinx. She also expressed her thinking that it was time for women to exercise their power in their communities and philanthropy.

In short, what Ponchitta aptly expressed is that social issues most

---

69 "Making a Difference in Racial Equity: Walmart C.E.O. Doug McMillon's Full Remarks," Walmart, https://corporate.walmart.com/equity

70 "Corporate Donations Tracker: Here Are The Companies Giving Millions To Anti-Racism Efforts," Isabele Togoh, Forbes, June 3, 2020, https://www.forbes.com/sites/isabeltogoh/2020/06/01/corporate-donations-tracker-here-are-the-companies-giving-millions-to-anti-racism-efforts/

71 "How the president of the Ford Foundation would reimagine the economy," David Brancaccio and Rose Conlon, Marketplace, July 2, 2020, https://www.marketplace.org/2020/07/02/ford-foundation-darren-walker-charitable-organizations-philanthropy-economy-social-bonds/

certainly impact philanthropy. Therefore, it's impossible to continue relying on dated and tired approaches that worked in the past, but no longer do today because of a digitally and tech-savvy, highly connected, and socially conscious world.

Innovation: The Key Ingredient

As you've probably noticed, the 21st Century has brought incredible world innovations. Before the 2000s, there was no iPhone or phones with cameras or Facebook and other social media platforms. Remember, or imagine that? We speak to our smart devices in our homes and offices, and our dependence on digital assistants only increases exponentially year after year.

We are in the midst of the digital revolution, where the world is moving from analog and mechanical technologies to digital electronics. Consequently, the digital revolution has brought about meaningful changes in how the world communicates, works, lives, and looks to resolve challenges. In other words, we're immersed in a digital world of a vastly powerful technology that brings all of the human knowledge to our fingertips through search engines. We have powerful artificial intelligence, and some hypothesize that in 20 years, we will experience a technological singularity where the development of technology is both irreversible and uncontrollable. All of this information and shared communication has caused profound changes in society and philanthropy.

Because of it, innovation is an essential idea or ingredient that business and nonprofit leaders must possess. Specific to the social good sector, volunteers, supporters, and donors understand how technology and the digital revolution has changed the game. They know or at least have an idea (not even brilliant scientists fully understand where technology is taking humans) of the humanity shifting power technology possesses. Supporters across the entire donor cycle understand the world we all share. As a result, they know that the ideas of innovation and disruption are not limited to the business world. They expect innovation to happen in the nonprofit industry.

Patty McDonough Kennedy, Founder & CEO of SpeakWell, which does online learning for kids K-8, is a noted female disruptor. She's been featured on TEDx, and the 7th-grade kids of the program she runs were the first in the nation to each deliver a TEDx talk. She commented on philanthropy today, *"The world is changing, and everyone has to get used to being comfortable with being uncomfortable. Our supporters and parents love this program because society is such that we are giving a voice to kids today. Their voice matters. It's not just the adults' voices, and that's why we managed to get the students to speak at TEDx. As we expand our program, we have corporate partners, parents, and supporters who think everyone's voice matters, and they want to hear what the future—Generation Z—has to say."*

As I mentioned, we have seen significant innovation occur in the nonprofit sector. As an example, we have charity:water and The Pool it created for the benefit of compensating its team. They decided that ensuring a market-based solution would result in higher employee retention. We have blockchain platforms such as BitGive and PinkCoin that bring that technology to donors, which allows them to see transparent results better.

Remember, there is a thought in the public that nonprofits have not been open enough in demonstrating how the fundraising dollars they receive makes a social impact that is measurable and scalable. As a fundraiser, I have spoken to many donors who don't think nonprofits are leaders in addressing the social problems that have plagued society for generations. With technology, it's getting a lot tougher for nonprofits that stick to old approaches that can succeed.

Further, you have for-profit businesses that have fully embraced making a social impact. As I mentioned earlier in this book, the Business Roundtable companies, such as Apple, JPMorgan Chase, and Amazon, have stated they are moving from a singular focus on shareholder profits. They also seek to invest in their employees, fighting climate change, and dealing fairly with third-party vendors.

During the time I was in the process of writing this book, sure enough, Jeff Bezos, CEO, Amazon committed $10 billion to fight climate change.[72] Although it is not the most significant philanthropic gift, that honor goes to Warren Buffet when he donated $37 billion to the Bill and Melinda Gates Foundation; it is still immensely substantial. Bezos' donation also demonstrates donor leadership in the face of an existential threat to humanity with climate change.

Moreover, 2020 has caused tremendous and accelerated changes in American and global societies. The pandemic caused whole industries, including the philanthropic sector, to go virtual as technology becomes wholly ingrained in every aspect of our personal, work, and social lives.

---

72 "Jeff Bezos Commits $10 Billion to Address Climate Change," Karen Weise, The New York Times, https://www.nytimes.com/2020/02/17/technology/jeff-bezos-climate-change-earth-fund.html?auth=login-email&login=email

Movements such as Black Lives Matter and Me Too, which spread virally and quickly because of technology, have caused monumental social shifts. As a result, whole segments of people who have felt disenfranchised before have stood up to say they will be heard. Corporations, businesses, and of course, nonprofits have to respond to all that is happening. It's impossible not to!

For nonprofits, what do all of these activities tell us about donors? They go to prove that donors—with their philanthropic money—are leaders in philanthropy. For the most part, it's not the charities, and the public and donors know it. How could that be possible when fully, 41.54 percent of nonprofits have budgets of less than $100,0000?[73] An additional 11.63 percent have budgets of less than $500,000 (totaling 53.17 percent of all nonprofits). Donors understand that on a nonprofit by nonprofit basis, that's not a lot of money, and it rarely—if ever—drives scalable innovation and change.

In short, people are tired. They don't want to hear about change or have more dialogue about how things will get better. They want to see the change—now. In fact, many donors tell me that they are more interested in giving to a cause over a particular charity. As we've seen in this book, that's fair because people are passionate about whatever they care about, but donors are much more flexible about how they seek to support a good cause. Again, it doesn't have to be through a particular charity or nonprofit. It could be through one of many tools, platforms, and organizations available to them thanks to technology's power.

So, as a fundraiser, I'm going to close this book with words from my friend, Alan Petelinsek, CEO, Power Test, Inc. I think he summed up this chapter and what every fundraiser needs to do to be meaningfully engaged in the future of fundraising, which has arrived. Here's what Alan said, "*Learn who your donors are and what they love... it's not what we want, but what we believe in that matters.*"

---

73 "How Big Are Most Non-Profits?" ZipSprout, https://zipsprout.com/how-big-are-most-non-profits/

ABOUT THE AUTHOR

Paul D'Alessandro, J.D., CFRE, is the founder and chairman of High Impact Nonprofit Advisors (HNA), and also D'Alessandro, Inc. (DAI), which is a fundraising and strategic management consulting company with more than 30 years of experience in the philanthropic sector. He has worked with hundreds of nonprofits to raise over a billion dollars for his clients in the U.S. and abroad. In addition, as a nonprofit and business expert who is also a practicing attorney, Paul has worked with high-level global philanthropists vetting and negotiating their strategic gifts to charitable causes. Paul understands that today's environment requires innovation and fresh thinking, which is why he recently launched HNA to train and coach leaders who want to make a difference in the world.

Made in the USA
Monee, IL
13 March 2021

62686173R00085